Why Do I *Always Feel* Guilty?

BREAKING FREE FROM WHAT WEIGHS YOU DOWN

MARY WHELCHEL

HARVEST HOUSE PUBLISHERS

EUGENE, OREGON

Cover by Koechel Peterson & Associates, Inc., Minneapolis, Minnesota

Cover photo © JLP / Sylvia Torres / Corbis; Back cover author photo © David DeJong

WHY DO I ALWAYS FEEL GUILTY?
Copyright © 2007 by Mary Whelchel
Published by Harvest House Publishers
Eugene, Oregon 97402
www.harvesthousepublishers.com

Library of Congress Cataloging-in-Publication Data
Whelchel, Mary.
  Why do I always feel guilty? / Mary Whelchel
     p. cm.
  ISBN-13: 978-0-7369-1890-9
  ISBN-10: 0-7369-1890-6
  1. Guilt—Religious aspects—Christianity. 2. Forgiveness—Religious aspects—Christianity.
  3. Forgiveness of sin. 4. Women—Religious Life I. Title.
  BT722.W52 2007
  248.8'43—dc22
                                                                    2006022301

Printed in the United States of America

07 08 09 10 11 12 13 14 15 / BP-SK / 10 9 8 7 6 5 4 3 2

To my pastor, Dr. Erwin Lutzer,
and the elders of The Moody Church,
for allowing me to develop my gifts in the church
and encouraging me through more than
25 years of ministry together.

Contents

The Truth Can
Set You Free

Why would you want to read a book about guilt? You wouldn't
...unless you're sick and tired of feeling guilty all too often and you'd
like to have a day or two once in a while that's free of struggles with
guilt feelings.

If ever there was a universal emotion that plagues almost every
thinking, caring person, guilt is it! I wonder how many hours I've
wasted, how many opportunities I've missed, how much joy and
peace I've forfeited because I felt guilty. Only God knows, but if the
records were revealed, I'm sure the truth would shock me.

I began to focus on my own struggle with guilt a few years ago as
I wrote a Bible study called *The Superwoman Complex*. As I encour-
aged women to see that God has not called us to be superwomen,
I had to address the guilt we women carry because of our mistaken
assumption that we must be all things to all people. But it was easier
for me to write about that than it was to remove the guilt feelings
from my mind and heart.

In my ministry to women over the past 25 years, God has often
made me deal with issues in my own life by bringing them to my
attention through other women in general. In this case I simply had
lived with my guilt, managing to suppress it whenever it surfaced,
but never being able to break free from its entanglements until I
was forced to confront it as I wrote that Bible study.

I would love to report that I now have total victory over feelings of guilt. But that is not true, and you wouldn't believe me anyway! But I *can* report that I have begun to recognize guilt for the satanic weapon that it is, and I have become intentional about disentangling it from my thought life and my emotions. Making me feel guilty had been an easy target for the enemy's attacks, but now by God's grace I am shoring up that vulnerable spot, and he's having a much more difficult time drowning me in guilt than he used to.

If you sense a need to take the offense against the onslaught of guilt in your own life, or perhaps you want to be able to help others who are struggling with guilt, I believe you'll find this book helpful and encouraging. It's not "pie in the sky someday by and by," but it presents God's truth about guilt, and that truth can set us free.

1

Can We Live
Guilt-free Lives?

GUILT...oh, how I hate that word! My life has been hounded with guilt. Why?

> Because of my past.
>
> Because many people think I'm nicer than I really am.
>
> Because I don't live up to my own expectations.
>
> Because I automatically accept blame.
>
> Because I'm not the perfect mother—or daughter, or sister, or friend.
>
> Because I don't consistently practice all that I preach.
>
> Because women are easy targets for guilt.

How long a list would you like? And I'm certain you could add your own unique sources of guilt to mine. In fact, a few of my girlfriends shared some of their guilts with me:

- "One thing that makes me feel guilty is giving in to fear and allowing fear to stop me from doing things—even things that the Lord wants me to do."

- "I have felt guilty for many years about working when my oldest daughter was young. I've always thought I did not feel as close to her as I do to my other kids and I have always blamed myself for not staying home with her when she was young."

- "I have felt guilty about not spending enough time playing, reading to, and simply having fun with my kids. I realize now that much of my life was very difficult and I never learned how to relax and simply have fun as much as I should have. Consequently, I have not done this as much with my kids, because I simply did not know how."

- "I carry the most guilt over things that can't be changed— opportunities I missed. Especially right now, with my children growing up—I mean, I never took them to the Grand Canyon. If I want to, I can linger for days on never having taken my children to the Grand Canyon and totally forget all the things I did do with them."

- "My mom always felt guilty because my younger brother didn't have a younger sibling. Could she help that? Her doctor said no more. And yet she carried a lot of guilt."

- "Biggest guilt: That I am not a soul-winner. Another guilt is that I felt I was not doing enough for others. I might have missed the opportunity to bring a hot meal to a needy friend, or I wasn't able to contribute to a certain person who was raising support for missionary work."

- "In my life I've felt guilty about divorce. Let me just go ahead and put the big one up there—the one that makes me feel like I have a neon sign on my forehead that proclaims, 'Failure.'"

- "I feel guilty about wasting the years and gifts that God has given me by living a lukewarm kind of life. I have felt guilty about missing teachable moments with my daughters—about not finding the right words and not setting the perfect example, which would surely place them on a straighter path than the one I've walked."

- "I tend to feel guilty about the time we spend with my husband's mom. We visit her every other weekend and it is getting harder to go. His brother and sister put us (me) on a guilt trip, thinking we should go more."

- "Recently I was eating my hamburger and fries on my lunch break at a fast-food restaurant (and feeling a little guilty that I had strayed from my diet) when a homeless man came up to my table and begged me to buy him a burger just as I was taking a big bite out of mine. I felt bad for him, but at the same time I felt that the restaurant should not have allowed a homeless person to disturb me while I was eating. Besides, if I helped every homeless person that approached me, I would go broke. Well, after I left the restaurant, I felt guilty for not buying the man a lunch. That's my guilt trip for the day."

- "I feel especially guilty when I worry and then eat instead of turning my anxiety over to God. I also struggle with guilt over how I use my time. For some reason, I feel that my minutes have to be productive, that I have to always be doing something. I have trouble granting myself time to just be."

This is just a small sampling of the guilts my good friends struggle with. And I can assure you that each of these women is outstanding in her own right, with many accomplishments and lots of spiritual maturity. Yet they still struggle with guilt.

There are few days in our lives that are guilt-free. For far too many of us, our days are filled with guilt.

Living with Guilt

A life burdened under a load of guilt is not the abundant life that Jesus came to give us. Guilt steals our joy, hinders our productivity, interrupts our peace, harms our relationships, and worst of all, makes us self-focused. When I'm feeling guilty, I'm thinking about myself; and when I think about myself very much, it always leads to dissatisfaction and discontent.

My niece put it this way: "Guilt certainly causes me to lose perspective and it almost always involves self. I can think I am totally over something, and then I can watch a movie or read a story or just have gloomy weather and get sucked right back into it. My feelings cannot be trusted."

Many of us continue to be loaded down with guilt because we feel guilty if we don't feel guilty! We assume that, knowing ourselves as we do, we deserve to feel guilty, so we accept it as our due punishment. We let guilt creep into our lives until it becomes part of the fabric of our personalities. We're so accustomed to living with guilt that it becomes our daily companion and we no longer recognize the evil and harm that it causes. How many of us say, "I'm sorry" as an automatic response, assuming guilt without any reason?

It is little wonder that the enemy of our souls, Satan himself, wields this weapon of guilt so broadly and with such effectiveness. He has long since recognized how easily we put up with guilt and how difficult it is for us to dump it. He knows that if he can keep us guilt-ridden, he can keep us from realizing God's potential for our lives. He wants to keep us from doing all the good things which God planned in advance for us to do, as stated in Ephesians 2:10. He effectively handicaps us so that our light doesn't shine so brightly and our testimony to God's grace is diminished.

While Satan may not be able to trip us up with some addiction or impurity or disgraceful public sin, it's not that difficult for him to bombard our minds with guilt. Many of us have grown in our faith to the point that we recognize and avoid some of the more obvious temptations. For Satan to try to tempt us to, say, have an affair, while not impossible, would require an incredible amount of effort on his part. Not so with guilt! When just one person looks at us the wrong way, we tend to take on guilt. When we fail to jump through someone else's hoop, suddenly we're guilt-ridden. When we succumb to one memory of sins in the past, guilt moves in. And because it is guilt, we fail to see it as a tool of Satan.

What Is Guilt?

Guilt is both a fact and a feeling. It is possible to be guilty without feeling guilty. It is possible to feel guilty without being guilty. And obviously, it is possible to be guilty and feel guilty. No doubt we have all experienced these three conditions.

Being guilty without feeling guilty can be due to ignorance. The apostle Paul wrote, "My conscience is clear, but that does not make me innocent. It is the Lord who judges me" (1 Corinthians 4:4). I may be guilty of breaking a law because I am ignorant of the law. For example, if I drive 40 miles per hour in a 30 miles-per-hour zone, I am guilty even though I think the speed limit is 40 miles per hour. My protests to the nice officer who is writing me a speeding ticket will fall on deaf ears because ignorance of the law is no excuse. I am still guilty.

If you are a Christian, it is not God's will for you to live in guilt.

It is also quite possible to have a hardened heart that feels no guilt even when we are guilty. Hebrews 3:13 admonishes us not to be "hardened by sin's deceitfulness." I may drive at an excessive speed—even though I know I am breaking the law—without feeling a tinge of guilt because I've become hardened to breaking that law to the point I no longer feel guilty, even though I am. (And just writing that paragraph makes me feel guilty, since I am guilty of having done this!)

Feeling guilty even when we are not guilty is a more common struggle for most of us. This false guilt is caused by wrong thinking. We feel guilty because we allow ourselves to think thoughts that tell us it is our fault, whatever "it" is. In this condition, we ignore the facts, we wallow in self-recrimination, and we send ourselves into a downward spiral of despair and discouragement without justification. That's because this false guilt is a feeling, not reality.

It has been said that feelings have zero IQ. That means they're not smart, and in dealing with my own feelings, I have found this to frequently be the case. My feelings can mislead me because they are often not based on reality. But feelings can be very strong and convincing, whether accurate or not.

By contrast, feeling guilty when we *are* guilty is a good thing! Hopefully that true guilt will cause us to repent and make needed changes.

To answer the question, Why do I always feel guilty? we are going to examine guilt feelings and their causes. We must learn to differentiate between true guilt and false guilt, and that can only be done by using the yardstick of God's Word.

Living Guilt-free

If you are a Christian, it is not God's will for you to live in guilt. Allowing guilt to continue to plague you is evidence that you are living a defeated life, and we Christians are called to live victoriously. Galatians 5:1 says, "It is for freedom Christ has set us free; stand firm, then, and do not let yourselves be burdened again by a yoke of slavery." To live with a constant feeling of guilt is to live with a yoke of slavery. It is to allow the feelings of guilt to choke the very life out of us. And Jesus came to set us free from this yoke.

The question I posed in the title of this chapter is, Can we live guilt-free lives? If you're talking about totally guilt-free, never having to deal with false guilt again, forever banishing guilt from your mind and heart, the answer is no—not on this side of heaven, not as long as we are still residing in earthly bodies that are burdened with that old nature of sin.

It's been interesting to note the reaction I've received from friends and acquaintances when I mention to them the title of this book. This is the fourteenth book I've written, and without question, the title—*Why Do I Always Feel Guilty?*—has generated more response than the title of any other book I've written. Common responses include, "I need to read that book," or "I could write that book." Most everyone readily relates to the topic of guilt, and this seemed to be true regardless of age or level of spiritual maturity or experience or personality.

And in the process of writing this book, I've come to the conclusion that living totally guilt-free is a nice cliché, but rarely achievable for any length of time. In fact, I'd be suspicious of anyone who tried to convince me they were living a totally guilt-free life. I might wonder if that person is in denial or simply refusing to face reality.

But what I do firmly believe is that we can live free from the constant plague of guilt. We can learn to recognize and manage our feelings of guilt, and we can get better and better at dealing with them. As one friend put it, "Guilt is sort of like mold on cheese. If it's not dealt with, the mold spreads, takes over, and renders the entire cheese unusable, worthless, disgusting. You have to cut the mold off as soon as you see it and throw it away to get back to the good stuff."

I am convinced that through the power of God's Spirit within us, as believers in Jesus Christ, we can learn to effectively and quickly cut off the mold of guilt before it overtakes us. We can learn to reject those messages of guilt that try to envelop our minds and flood our thoughts and rob us of the freedom that is ours in Christ.

We have to learn how to refuse to submit to the yoke of guilt. We must learn to recognize Satan's strategy and stand firm against it. It's time we discover that guilt is not meant to be part of our everyday living; it is not normal; it is not okay; it is not inevitable.

But, you're thinking, *that is easier said than done.* Of course it's easier said than done! What isn't? But that's no excuse for not doing it. If you're tired of the yoke of guilt and ready to live in the freedom that Christ came to give us, I encourage you to keep reading. It *is* possible to learn to deal with your guilt feelings and keep them from occupying your mind. We have power to do it because we as Christians have God's Spirit in us.

As one who has struggled through lots of guilt in my own life and allowed it to keep me down far too long, I have written this book to share with you some biblical principles and truths that have begun to set me free. I say "begun" because this is a lifelong lesson and pursuit. But I am beginning to learn to manage and deal with those feelings of guilt, and discovering the incredible joy it brings. More than that, it sets me free to worship God more fully and to know Him more deeply. It sets me free from self-absorption and allows me to focus on serving others.

I would love to help you make progress along this path of guilt-free living, and it is my prayer that this book will do just that!

2

Confronting
True Guilt

If we ever hope to manage our guilt, we must learn to recognize the difference between true guilt and false guilt. Sometimes it is a very thin line between the two, and until we know how to tell the difference, we'll not be able to adequately deal with our feelings of guilt.

In one sense, it's easier to deal with true guilt than with false. That's because we can put our finger on the cause of the true guilt, and there's usually little doubt about what we need to do. The big struggle with true guilt is relinquishing our will and giving up our rights and saying yes to the convicting voice of God's Spirit.

My Ten-Year Burden

True guilt is what we feel when God convicts us of some area in our life that needs to be changed, and we are resisting that change. And the longer we resist obeying God, the heavier the burden of true guilt becomes. This is not because God is dumping guilt on us. Rather it is because we haven't chosen to obey quickly and decisively.

For ten long years I carried around true guilt. I decided that I wanted to run my own life, pursue my own goals, and do my own thing. Mind you, I had no excuse for the selfish and sinful choices I made, but in spite of biblical knowledge and support from Christian family and friends, I was convinced that God's way would take me where I didn't want to go. So, God was relegated to the backseat of my life and I ran the show.

My father's nickname for me was *Hardhead* because (like him) I was—and am—a very determined person. I don't give up easily. That's a good trait when it is under the control of the Holy Spirit, but left to its own devices, it is dangerous. So, this pursuit of happiness and fulfillment on which I was engaged rarely ever yielded anything more than temporary pleasure. Nonetheless, I kept on that wayward path for a long time.

Remembering those days, I can again feel that burden of true guilt, which was my constant companion. I used many devices to escape it and deny it and bury it, but it was always there. Busyness was my most common diversion tactic; if I just kept moving, always doing something, then there wouldn't be time to think, because when I was alone with my thoughts, guilt flooded my mind. And there was no ambiguity as to why I felt guilty. I knew there was sin and rebellion in my life, and I knew it was wrong.

It took ten long years, but I finally traveled down that evil path until I reached its end. There was simply nowhere else to turn. I could no longer deny that my way was a disaster; and because I was truly a child of God, even through those awful years, I knew that my only hope for peace was to get right with God. And getting right with God meant confessing my sin, acknowledging my guilt, and begging for forgiveness.

After a three-day inner struggle, with practically no sleep and terrible turmoil, I gave up and allowed God to take charge of my shattered, frazzled life. Immediately the peace of God returned to my heart. Knowing my sins were forgiven and that I now had open communication with my heavenly Father was such a relief of mind and heart. I had forgotten what it was like to be rid of true guilt. I never realized how heavy that burden had become until it was gone.

I still had much to learn, and each day for a long time I had to recommit myself to God's control because old habits die hard, and

I was walking away from a deeply cherished dream. But each day I grew stronger, and the grace of God began to work miracles in me. With true guilt off my back, I was free to think about other people and start serving God wholeheartedly with the gifts and opportunities He gave me. I was beginning to live guilt-free!

True Guilt's Long History

True guilt goes back to the Garden of Eden. From the moment Adam and Eve sinned, guilt entered the picture. Their immediate reaction was a result of guilt; they tried to hide themselves and cover up their sin. They made excuses and shifted the blame. True guilt broke their fellowship with God and brought great loss into their lives.

Adam and Eve's immediate response to true guilt is typical. Most of us do the same when we are forced to face our failings. We go into cover-up mode; we rationalize it away; we blame someone or something else. One way to identify true guilt is to take a look at your initial reaction when confronted with your wrongdoing. Cover-up and denial are symptomatic of true guilt.

The Effects of True Guilt

True guilt not only affects our feelings, but can affect our physical health, too. In Psalm 38 we find one of Scriptures' most vivid descriptions of the effects of true guilt. King David felt guilty because he had done wrong, and notice the toll his guilt took on him:

> O LORD, do not rebuke me in your anger or discipline me in your wrath. For your arrows have pierced me, and your hand has come down upon me. Because of your wrath there is no health in my body; my bones have no soundness because of my sin. My guilt has overwhelmed me like a burden too heavy to bear. My wounds fester and are loathsome because of my sinful folly. I am bowed down and brought very low; all day long I go about mourning. My back is filled with searing pain; there is

no health in my body. I am feeble and utterly crushed; I
groan in anguish of heart. All my longings lie open before
you, O Lord; my sighing is not hidden from you. My
heart pounds, my strength fails me; even the light has
gone from my eyes (Psalm 38:1-10).

King David had been harboring this true guilt for months. He
was guilty of a great sin—actually, a whole string of sins. Second
Samuel 11 relates the whole sad story to us—of how David's lust
led to adultery, which led to deception, which eventually led to
murder. No doubt it never entered David's mind that his invitation
to Bathsheba for a one-night stand would lead to these dreadful
choices on his part.

That's why Proverbs 4:14 says, "Do not set foot on the path of
the wicked or walk in the way of evil men." It's the first step on a
treacherous path that leads us toward a downward spiral, and King
David's decision to take a step onto the slippery slope toward evil
brought him to disaster.

David's words in Psalm 38 describe the pain of true guilt. He
said, "There is no health in my body; my bones have no soundness
because of my sin." He described festering wounds and backaches;
he had heart trouble and his eyesight was failing him. Literal physical ailments and conditions were the result of this true guilt that
David experienced.

I wonder how many of our physical problems are caused by true
guilt? Could it be that the headaches and backaches and heart conditions and high-blood pressure some of us experience are caused
by true guilt that has not been dealt with? It's common knowledge
that our physical conditions are inextricably connected with our
emotional and mental conditions.

And of course, King David was plagued with emotional and
mental pain, too. His words graphically describe that pain:

"I am bowed down and brought very low; all day long I
go about mourning."

" I am feeble and utterly crushed; I groan in anguish of heart."

"…my sighing is not hidden from you."

This is a man in deep depression, a man at the end of his physical and emotional rope. True guilt has driven him into a terrible state of despair. He says, "My guilt has overwhelmed me like a burden too heavy to bear."

True guilt is too heavy for us, too. Whether we harbor a huge guilt like David's or just keep refusing to face the "little stuff" in our lives that needs to be cleaned up, that true guilt will eventually take its toll on us and cause us mental, emotional, and physical suffering.

God's Remedy for True Guilt

In the Old Testament era, God established a means by which the Israelites could alleviate their guilt by sacrificing a perfect ram (Leviticus 5:14–6:7). The people had to make this guilt offering each time they broke the law and sinned so that they could live without guilt. God provided a way for His people to get rid of their guilt, even if it was only temporary, because He didn't want them to live with the burden of guilt.

> Romans 8:1 says, "There is now no condemnation for those who are in Christ Jesus."

The same is true today. Our heavenly Father does not want us to live with the burden of guilt, but we don't need guilt offerings any longer. The incredible good news of the gospel is that Jesus came to offer Himself as the perfect sacrifice and become our once-and-for-all guilt offering. Hebrews 10:12 says, "When [Christ] had offered for all time one sacrifice for sins, he sat down at the right hand of God." We now have a way to deal with true guilt because Jesus paid the price. Through His sacrifice on Calvary for us, He has provided the way of escape from our true guilt.

Are You Harboring True Guilt?

Are you carrying a heavy load of true guilt because you have never accepted the sacrifice that Jesus made for the forgiveness of your sins and the removal of your guilt?

Romans 8:1 says, "There is now no condemnation for those who are in Christ Jesus." These are some of the most glorious words in the Bible—no condemnation! Jesus died to take away your true guilt. If you've never confessed that you are a sinner and you need the forgiveness of God, if you've never personally accepted Jesus as your Savior, if you don't know that peace with God which comes with forgiveness of your sins, I want to encourage you to do that right now. You'll never get rid of true guilt until you accept the sacrifice for your guilt that Jesus provided. To find out how you can do this, see the appendix on page 155.

However, even after we become a Christian and are born from above, we will experience true guilt whenever we sin against the Lord. Anytime we sin and refuse to confess and forsake our sin, we heap true guilt on ourselves.

Recognizing True Guilt

For each of us, guilt will have varying effects and symptoms. But here are some distinguishing characteristics—telltale signs—of true guilt that are generally true for all of us:

- *You know exactly what the cause is.*

  It is not a mystery to you. The convicting voice of God's Spirit makes it abundantly clear that you are not living in obedience. It is specific and you can put your finger on it. Whether it is large or small, short term or long term, clearly visible or hidden, it is no secret to you.

  For many years I was fairly adept at hiding my guilt from others. I didn't talk about it around my Christian friends; I put on the right face and did the right things to keep them from knowing about my "double life." But never for a moment was I confused about the cause of my feelings of guilt.

- *You know what you should do.*

Since the cause of true guilt is clear, the course of action is also. No one has to tell you what you need to do—though God often uses others to bring us to the place where we are willing to face the cause of our guilt.

In my case, I closed my ears to any convicting voice for several years, but toward the end, God put me in a church under the preaching of a man of God and that began to bring me to the end of my rope. I knew what I had to do; it was a matter of my willingness to do it.

- *You may try to rationalize the sin away, or shift the blame, but that doesn't work.*

Like Adam and Eve, most of us spend a good bit of time trying to convince ourselves that what we're doing isn't really that bad. We compare ourselves to others and decide we're not nearly as guilty as they are. We rationalize that our good traits offset the bad ones. We try to shift the blame to our environment, or our upbringing, or our circumstances, or some other person.

In those alone moments when I could not escape my thoughts, I would do my best to believe that I had a right to do what I was doing. After all, I told myself, there were good reasons for it. And I gravitated toward people—not Christians—who validated that point of view. In fact, I had friends who told me what I was doing was normal, no big deal. I held at arm's length the friends who would have held me accountable. But never did I escape the knowing in the depth of my being that I was truly guilty and there was no one to blame but myself.

Freedom from True Guilt

If you recognize some true guilt in your life, I hope you won't take as long as I did to deal with it. You don't need ten more minutes of carrying around true guilt, much less ten years! It's a burden that is far too heavy, and as was true with me, you may not even realize how heavily it is weighing on you.

The first step to freedom is to acknowledge to God why you feel guilty. But please don't stop there. Go on to accept God's forgiveness. He is a compassionate and loving God, and He longs to take that burden of true guilt off of you and give you the freedom you desire. Remember, He is our heavenly Father and He is a perfect Father. His plans for you are good and peaceful, but that load of true guilt will get in your way of realizing His goodness.

If you continue to harbor that sin and refuse to obey, as I did for ten long years, then guilt will continue to invade your mind and destroy your peace. God will press His case with you, convicting you, in order to get you to move quickly and not stay in that unforgiven condition any longer.

Many people continue to carry around true guilt because they refuse to accept responsibility for their own actions. Or they refuse to face the problem and they keep sticking their head in the sand like an ostrich, acting like it's nothing important and hoping that, given enough time, it will go away. But no matter how small the problem may seem to you, the guilt will grow and grow until you confess, forsake, own up, and stop making excuses.

The same King David who was tortured with true guilt in Psalm 38 eventually confessed his sin and found forgiveness. And he describes the great relief that comes through such surrender:

> Blessed is he whose transgressions are forgiven, whose sins are covered. Blessed is the man whose sin the LORD does not count against him and in whose spirit is no deceit. When I kept silent, my bones wasted away through my groaning all day long. For day and night your hand was heavy upon me; my strength was sapped as in the heat of summer. Then I acknowledged my sin to you and did not cover up my iniquity. I said, "I will confess my transgressions to the LORD"—and you forgave the guilt of my sin (Psalm 32:1-5).

As long as David harbored sin and didn't confess it to God, the guilt continued to plague his conscience. God kept His hand heavy on David until he acknowledged his guilt.

God wasn't being cruel to David. Rather, out of love, He was trying to get David to act quickly, confess his sin, and find forgiveness. And the same is true for us. Until we confess, true guilt will never leave us. God allows true guilt to continue so that it will pressure us into turning away from that which is wrong and seeking His righteousness.

Freedom from true guilt begins with acknowledging your sin— admitting to God the reason for the guilt. If you're ready to do that, then you're ready to get rid of a very heavy burden. And I promise you, that burden of true guilt is much heavier than you realize until you unload it.

As I look back on my ten-year burden of true guilt, I wonder why it took me so long to recognize the foolishness of my reluctance to deal with it. Hopefully you are not as hardheaded as I am—or was—and you will not wait to deal with whatever true guilt is now heavy on your heart. As in the story of the prodigal son, you have a heavenly Father who is waiting with open arms, who will indeed rush to meet you as soon as you turn your face toward home and return to the only place where you can find forgiveness and peace.

Growing Free from Guilt

1. Before you begin this exercise, pray that God will shine His light of truth into your heart and make you willing and able to recognize any true guilt you find there. Then note below any known area(s) of true guilt in your life.

   _____

   _____

   _____

   _____

   _____

2. Now, look at each one of these guilts you've identified as true, and ask yourself the following questions about each one:

   - Is this an area of disobedience? That is, am I not obeying what God has clearly shown me?
   - If so, why have I refused to obey God? What fears or stubbornness on my part is keeping me from doing what I know God wants me to do?
   - Do I really want to get rid of this true guilt?
   - What exact steps will I have to take to get rid of this true guilt?
   - Have I tried in the past to obey God in this area and failed? Why?
   - Have I gone to God for forgiveness and acknowledged that I have been forgiven?

   If you have already been forgiven for something on your list yet the guilt seems to linger on, then cross this item off and write beside it, "Forgiven—no more guilt."

   I encourage you not to hesitate in dealing with true guilt. It may appear that the steps required are too drastic, too costly. But nothing is more costly in the long term than refusing to deal with known areas of sin or disobedience. Remember, God is eagerly waiting to take away that true guilt and extend His forgiveness to you as soon as you are ready to repent and obey.

3

What Is
False Guilt?

After a recent operation, under orders from her doctor to do absolutely nothing for several weeks, my good friend Betsy shared her feelings of guilt with me. Mind you, Betsy is one of the most active, giving, involved people you will ever find, with a long list of accomplishments and service to her church, her family, her friends, her Christian school, and her community. But in spite of all that, she writes:

> Guilt—the gift that keeps on giving. I sit here and see everyone doing things for me and caring for me and think about all the ways people are serving those who are less fortunate, and guilt is beginning to build up. Even when I know I'm not in control of this particular situation, it still is there because I have time to ponder how I generally spend my time, and the things other people do seem so much more worthy.

This is a good example of false guilt. Betsy acknowledges in her mind that this is beyond her control, yet the guilty feelings still move in. Notice also that as she had more time to think about herself, she began to experience more false guilt.

Another woman told me that her former husband went on a

business trip, met a young woman who captured his fancy, and just that quickly, without any warning, came home to tell her that he didn't love her any longer and wanted a divorce. After over 20 years of marriage, he made an overnight decision to go for the young gal. And then he had the nerve to tell my friend, "You just weren't a good wife." She looked at me and said, "I thought I was a good wife, but I guess I wasn't."

Her husband blamed her for his affair and the divorce, and she accepted the blame, which led to feelings of false guilt. Though she had done nothing wrong, she was feeling guilty. That story could be multiplied many times, in one form or another. Women are particularly prone to accept blame without reason. If accused, we tend to respond with "guilty as charged," even when we are not.

Self-imposed Guilt

False guilt is a guilt we impose upon ourselves. We allow it to take root in our minds, to start causing all kinds of bad feelings, to feed us all kinds of lies, and we begin to believe it. If we learn to recognize false guilt, to address it head-on, and to practice biblical principles that will drive out the false guilt, we can get rid of it. That's why I say it is self-imposed guilt. So, there—you have something else to feel guilty about: that you allow yourself to feel guilty when you shouldn't!

False guilt can be defined as…

- what we experience when we keep remembering what God has forgiven and forgotten.
- what we feel when someone appears to be disappointed in us.
- what we feel when we have to say no.
- what we feel when we try to please people and fail.
- what we feel when we live with unrealistic expectations of ourselves.
- what we feel when we allow others to dictate what and who we should be.

Notice that each item in that list begins with "what we experience" or "what we feel." It's a feeling not grounded in truth, but nonetheless strong and real. The feelings that result from both true and false guilt are very similar, and our challenge is to learn to discern the difference between them. We must learn to quickly analyze any guilt that comes our way: Is this true or false guilt? Have I done something I can specifically identify for which I deserve blame? Or is this just a nebulous feeling of guilt because I feel someone is unhappy with me, I feel I haven't measured up, or I am struggling with something totally beyond my control?

Signs of False Guilt

With true guilt you can often lay your finger on the exact cause, but that's not usually the case with false guilt. One of the first signs that you are dealing with false guilt is that you just can't pinpoint exactly why you feel guilty. It is a strong feeling that engulfs you and discourages you, but if you had to state why you feel guilty, you'd say things like, "Well, I just never seem to get it right," or "I don't know, I just should have known better," or "She's always telling me that I need to improve," or "I just can't seem to make anyone happy." Or like my friend Betsy, "Even though I know my current circumstance is beyond my control, I still feel guilty because I'm unable to do anything and others are doing things that are so much more worthy."

Notice how general those statements are. When you cannot pinpoint a specific reason for your guilt, it is highly likely you're dealing with false guilt.

Discerning False Guilt

Here are some illustrations of both true and false guilt. Read each one, and determine for yourself which are true guilt and which are false:

—My daughter said to me, "But all the other mothers will be

there. Why can't you be there?" I feel guilty because I can't be at her scout meeting.

—My boss said, "You don't have that report finished yet?" I feel guilty, but I haven't had time to breathe. My boss keeps interrupting me with other priorities, and then doesn't understand why everything doesn't get done on time.

—A good friend asked me if I would meet her for prayer. She's very worried about her mother, who is ill. I had made plans to go shopping, and told her I couldn't meet her tonight. I feel guilty.

—The committee chairperson at church called me at work to talk about an upcoming meeting. I told her I couldn't talk with her at that moment and would call her later in the evening. She sounded irritated. I feel guilty.

—I stopped going to church for six months a few years ago and got away from fellowship with the Lord. During that time, my lifestyle was not very Christlike. I feel very guilty about it.

—Before I became a Christian and was forgiven of my sins, I had an abortion, which I now deeply regret. Many nights I lie sleepless in bed, feeling so guilty about the baby I destroyed.

—My father died without becoming a believer. I think of the times I might have talked to him and didn't. Maybe it's my fault he never accepted Christ. I feel terribly guilty about it.

—I keep letting my quiet time with the Lord slip, finding one excuse after another. I feel guilty about it.

—I feel I should be doing some exercise to keep my body in good shape, but I hate to exercise. I feel guilty.

—I know my cholesterol is on the high side, but I find it difficult to stay away from the tasty stuff, such as butter and fried food and desserts. I feel guilty.

—I was abrupt and unkind to my mate this morning. I made a sarcastic comment that was unnecessary. I feel guilty.

—My sister just accused me of not spending enough time with

her. She feels we should get together every weekend, but I just don't have time. I feel guilty.

Let's look at some of these examples to get a better understanding of the differences between false versus true guilt.

Example #1: My daughter said to me, "But all the other mothers will be there. Why can't you be there?" I feel guilty because I can't be at her scout meeting.

Remember that kids are terrific at laying guilt on us. When your children use the "all the other mothers" line, or "everybody else is doing it," you know you're being attacked by kid guilt. This technique has been around for a long time and is widespread, so it goes with the territory of parenthood. Most kid guilt is false guilt.

Example #2: My boss said, "You don't have that report finished yet?" I feel guilty, but I haven't had time to breathe. My boss keeps interrupting me with other priorities, and then doesn't understand why everything doesn't get done on time.

We often allow our employers to place false guilt on us. Certainly those in authority over us have a right and a responsibility to correct us and direct us, but when that authority figure has unrealistic expectations, it can lead to lots of false guilt for us.

Example #3: A good friend asked me if I would meet her for prayer. She's very worried about her mother, who is ill. I had made plans to go shopping, and told her I couldn't meet her tonight. I feel guilty.

When a friend asks you to pray with her, that would typically have a higher priority than discretionary shopping. You might argue that you can't ignore some needed shopping and the prayer time can be postponed, which may be the case. But you would know if your decision to shop came from unwillingness on your part to change your plans and inconvenience yourself a bit.

Example #4: The committee chairperson at church called me at

> **If God can and does forgive us, then who are we not to forgive ourselves?**

work to talk about an upcoming meeting. *I told her I couldn't talk with her at that moment and would call her later in the evening. She sounded irritated. I feel guilty.*

If someone calls you at work on a personal issue and you don't have time to talk with that person, you should not feel guilty because he or she is irritated, provided you responded as nicely and gently as possible. But when people get irritated with us, we tend to take on guilt, don't we? Don't let someone's unhappiness with you cause you to take on false guilt. It's very possible, and quite often the case, that the other person's attitude is wrong.

Example #5: Before I became a Christian and was forgiven of my sins, I had an abortion, which I now deeply regret. Many nights I lie sleepless in bed, feeling so guilty about the baby I destroyed.

The false guilt many of us suffer from the most is guilt over things done long ago. We all tend to go back and remember the sins of the past, and even though they are forgiven and God remembers them no longer, we don't seem to be able to purge our memory.

This kind of false guilt requires much prayer, support from fellow-believers, and a constant reminder that God's forgiveness is complete, He remembers our past sins against us no more, and we are no longer condemned. If God can and does forgive us, then who are we not to forgive ourselves? We must forgive ourselves and refuse to be enslaved by this kind of false guilt.

One night on my way home, I was tired and my mind was wandering, and my foot got heavy on the accelerator. I was going 45 in a 30-mile-per-hour zone, and just two doors away from my home, I was stopped for speeding and a nice officer wrote me a ticket.

As he handed it to me, he said that because I had a clean record, I could sign a paper asking for court supervision, pay my $50 fine, and the speeding ticket would not show up on my record at all. He said, "There will be no record anywhere of this offense; it will be as though it never happened."

That's what God does for us, but we don't have to pay $50. By simple faith and confession on our part He blots out our transgressions, and He keeps no record of them. If you looked in His record books they wouldn't be there. He and anyone else in the heavenlies who has access to the books would tell you that it is as if no such offense was ever committed.

Oh, how we need to understand this beautiful truth and learn to let go of the guilt of forgiven sin, remembering there is now no condemnation for us.

Example #6: My father died without becoming a believer. I think of the times I might have talked to him and didn't. Maybe it's my fault he never accepted Christ. I feel terribly guilty about it.

Remember that anyone who seeks to know God will find Him. Even if we didn't do the best job in the world of witnessing to someone, if that person has a seeking heart, he or she will find the Lord. Now, that doesn't let us off the hook for our failure to be good witnesses, but if indeed you did fail to witness to someone who has since passed on, it is a sin that can be forgiven and the guilt doesn't have to weigh you down.

During my ten-year sabbatical from walking with the Lord, I had a very good friend with whom I worked, another single woman, and we were spending a short vacation together in Florida. As she was driving us to the beach one day, a 14-wheel semitruck pulled into our lane and hit us head-on. The driver's seat took most of the impact, and my friend died shortly after she was taken to the hospital.

Not only did I not witness to her as I should have, but I failed to live a pure life and present a godly example to her. That is a terrible indictment of my spiritual condition at that time, but it's been forgiven. I know from Scripture that my lack of witnessing did not determine her eternal destination; she made that choice. How I wish I could have shared my faith in Jesus with her; what a joy that would have been. But it is in the past, it is forgiven, it's no longer on the books against me, and I now refuse to allow it to plague my mind with guilt and regret. Obviously, I have not forgotten it; only God can purposely forget our sins. He alone has the ability to remember them no more. But I can still live free from the guilt of my failure.

Determining the Source of Our Guilt

Looking at some of the aforementioned examples, you'll notice that false guilt frequently comes from people who indicate their lack of satisfaction with us in some way. It is natural to feel guilty, but we need to mentally check the facts every time it happens. When someone says, "Why weren't you…" or "Why didn't you…" and you immediately start to feel guilty, remind yourself that it is highly likely you're dealing with false guilt.

I've had to learn to do this as I try to minister to people. I feel guilty when I don't have answers, when I can't come up with the right course of action and give them counsel that immediately makes them feel better.

Once I was speaking at a seminar and a woman came up to say that she was disappointed because I hadn't talked about empty nesters. Immediately I started to feel guilty over her disappointment, but very quickly I did a mental checkup and reminded myself that God had not laid it on my heart to talk about the problems of empty nesters, I don't even know what I would say about the subject, and I couldn't allow myself to feel guilty because I hadn't met her specific need. The fact that I didn't meet someone's needs doesn't mean I should feel guilty about it.

Recently a woman stopped me in church to ask for help in dealing with a rebellious teenage daughter. She was looking for a seminar on that topic. Since I am the director of women's ministries at my church, I want to be able to help any woman who comes to me about any particular topic. But I could not find what she wanted—a seminar for mothers with rebellious teenage daughters.

My first reaction was to blame myself. I thought *Why haven't you had a seminar on this topic? If you were doing your job as director of women's ministries, then you could meet her need.* I have an ever-present tendency to feel guilty when I cannot meet someone else's expectations. Having many years of experience with this kind of false guilt, I am learning to recognize it much more quickly now so that I can refuse to allow it to affect my thought life.

I did find some books to recommend to the woman, and when I called to share that information with her, she seemed very apprecia-tive for the information. As I hung up the phone, I thought about how pleased she seemed to be that I had at least tried. She wasn't dumping guilt on me. I believe that much of our false guilt is self-imposed. We imagine that others are blaming us, even when they are not.

Learning to Manage False Guilt

Not long ago a friend confronted me about something I had said which had hurt her feelings. Obviously I was very sorry to hear that my words had caused her some pain, and of course I apologized and accepted full responsibility. But I can tell you that I did not feel guilty about it. The reason was that my intentions and motivations were pure; I had no ill-feelings or desires in my heart to do harm, and in fact, I simply thought I had made a clever and funny com-ment and that she would understand it as such.

Why didn't I feel guilty? I had hurt her feelings, and as soon as this was brought to my attention, I apologized to her and then privately prayed to God for understanding of why my words had caused pain when I had never intended for them to do so. The Lord graciously revealed to me that I have to be careful with quips. Sometimes I can easily give a witty comeback to someone's com-ment, yet do so without thinking about how it might sound to the other person. (I think it's a result of being raised with brothers and spending most of my professional life with men, who use quips and barbs as a way of showing fondness and friendship. But that's generally not true with women.)

So, I've begun to pray about that and the Spirit of God has checked my spirit several times since then, reminding me to keep that quip to myself. I am grateful for the experience, because it has increased my sensitivity to others and helped me to make some needed changes. But I don't carry guilt over that incident because I had no bad intentions—just the opposite.

If this had happened some years earlier in my life, I would have lost many nights of sleep over it. I would have allowed the guilt to saturate my mind and my emotions for days or weeks. I would have relived it time and again, probably done some mental shifting of blame, and may have allowed it to cause a rift in our relationship. Fortunately, none of those things happened this time because I'm learning to deal with false guilt.

Managing False Guilt

The first and most important step in learning to manage false guilt is to recognize it. That is where we have the most trouble, because, remember, it usually feels just like true guilt. So we must develop the practice of examining our guilty feelings and determining whether we're experiencing true guilt or false. That will do more than anything else to help rid your mind of false guilt, because once you know the guilt is not deserved, it's much easier to put it out of your mind.

The second step is to replace wrong thinking with right thinking. When you're dealing with false guilt, you must, by choice, or by a set of your will, push that wrong thinking out of your mind. I emphasize "by a set of your will" because your feelings will take you in another direction. Setting your will is done by faith and in obedience to Scripture.

Philippians 4:8 gives us clear instructions on what kind of thoughts we need to cultivate in order to drive out wrong thinking. We are to think about things that are true, noble, right, pure, lovely, admirable, excellent, and praiseworthy. When we are feeling guilty undeservedly, we are allowing our minds to be filled with thoughts that are not true and certainly not lovely. So, you push those wrong thoughts out by thinking upon that which is true and lovely.

One way to do this is through praise to the Lord. Isaiah says we are kept in perfect peace when our minds are stayed on the Lord (Isaiah 26:3). Start counting your blessings. Begin thanking God for the good things in your life. Refuse to allow false guilt to have a place in your mind.

There Is No Condemnation!

I love the assurances in Romans 8:33-34 as stated in *The New Testament in Modern English* by J.B. Phillips:

> Who would dare to accuse us, whom God has chosen? The judge himself has declared us free from sin. Who is in a position to condemn? Only Christ, and Christ died for us, Christ rose for us, Christ reigns in power for us, Christ prays for us!

Only Christ is qualified to accuse us of wrong, and after we become Christians, He doesn't! Do we have a right to condemn ourselves if Jesus doesn't condemn us? And can anyone else truly condemn you if Jesus doesn't?

To condemn someone is, in today's vernacular, to "lay a guilt trip" on him. If we replace the word "condemn" with "lay a guilt trip," Romans 8:33-34 would read,

> Who would dare to accuse us, whom God has chosen? The judge himself has declared us free from sin. Who is in a position *to lay a guilt trip on us?* Only Christ, and Christ died for us, Christ rose for us, Christ reigns in power for us, Christ prays for us!

To allow ourselves to wallow in false guilt is to live in condemnation. It is the devil's trick, and I can imagine that God must shake

His head at those of us who, though we are forgiven, continue to live under the burden of false guilt.

Remember, if God is not condemning you, you have no reason to let anyone else condemn you—not even yourself. I would urge you to memorize Romans 8:1, "There is now no condemnation for those who are in Christ Jesus," and Isaiah 43:25: "I, even I, am he who blots out your transgressions, for my own sake, and remembers your sins no more."

So, don't live in condemnation. Stand up to the false guilt in your life and declare you are no longer under its power. It may be a bit of a journey to learn to manage that false guilt, and you may experience both success and failure as you head down that path, but don't be discouraged. There is great relief ahead as we stand firm in the freedom that Christ gives us and refuse to allow ourselves to be burdened again by a yoke of slavery (see Galatians 5:1).

In the chapters that follow, we will take an in-depth look at specific causes of false guilt. Since it isn't always easy to identify its sources, this will help you uncover any false guilt that may have become entrenched in your mind. That, then, will allow you to begin the process of getting rid of that false guilt and living in the freedom that is your birthright in Christ Jesus.

Growing Free from Guilt

1. Before beginning this exercise, ask God to reveal to you any false guilt you may be harboring. Then try to identify those times when you feel guilty but you don't know why. Also, identify situations or people or environments that tend to bring on feelings of false guilt.

   These are the times and situations when I feel guilty, but don't know exactly why:

   _____

   _____

   _____

   _____

   _____

2. Next, ask yourself these questions about those guilts you identified as false:

   • Why have I taken on this false guilt? What or who is the cause of it?

   • What experiences from my past are making me feel this undeserved guilt?

   • How long have I been struggling with this false guilt?

   • Is this a constant feeling of guilt or does it occur only occasionally?

   • Have I yet recognized that I have no reason to feel guilty about this, and if so, why do I continue to allow myself to feel guilty about it?

   • Have I ever prayed about this false guilt and asked God to deliver me from it? If so, why does it keep recurring?

   Depending on how long you've allowed your false guilts to stay around, it may take a while to get rid of them. But every time a false guilt starts to bombard your mind, stand right up to it, call it what it is—false guilt, and refuse to accept it. Many times I say out loud, "I refuse to take on this guilt. It is false; it is not from God." I find it helpful to verbalize my rejection of false guilt.

4

Men, Women, *and Guilt*

While speaking to a class of Christian college students recently, I asked the men in the class how they dealt with guilt. One or two of them began to describe true guilt:

> "I told a lie recently because I didn't want to hurt someone's feelings. But I knew I shouldn't have told that lie, and it really bothered me until I made it right."

> "I was rude to someone and it bugged me until I asked that person to forgive me."

When I asked the class about false guilt, the men looked at me with puzzled expressions. I tried to describe what false guilt was, and it was clear this was not something they struggled with. One young man reported that his father was always trying to lay a guilt trip on him because he didn't call him every day. "But," he said, "he knows my phone number. He can call me anytime he wants to. I just say, 'Sorry, Dad,' and let it go, but I don't really feel sorry."

By contrast, the women in the class had no difficulty understanding false guilt. They could give me many examples of it in their own lives. I didn't have to define it for them. But the men were clueless.

What does this tell us about men, women, and guilt? It's pretty clear that we handle guilt quite differently. But that should not surprise us, because God created us with different natures and we often respond in different ways to the world around us, especially where emotions are concerned—and guilt is an emotion.

Differences in Our Brains

Scientists have discovered that the left and right sides of our brains have unique functions. The left side is the analytical, reasoning, problem-solving side; the right side is the emotional, creative, impulsive side. Typically each individual tends to have a dominant side, to be either right-brained or left-brained, meaning we approach life either from the left side—analytically and rationally—or from the right side—creatively and emotionally. And most men are far more left-brained than right-brained.

You might jump to the conclusion that most women then are more right-brained, and indeed the stereotypes would cause you to believe that. Women are seen to be more emotional and excitable than men, and in fact, men often see this as a weakness in women. However, the female brain, unlike the male brain, has a bridge or connection between the two sides that gives women the ability to transition from right brain to left brain far more easily than men can make the transition from left to right.

You can see this played out in male and female behavior. Men can isolate their feelings and emotions in order to get a job done or solve a problem. They have the ability to remove the emotions from the equation and address a situation or problem in a purely cerebral manner. Women are more likely to get to that rational stage after going through the emotional stage first. We are generally more sensitive and tenderhearted, and we tend to take things personally, no matter how many times our male counterparts may exhort us not to!

It's not difficult to see why women struggle more with guilt than men do. Guilt is a feeling. We women tend to feel first and reason later. So we take on this feeling of guilt, assuming it is deserved because we feel it. Men tend to isolate those feelings, rationalize the guilt more quickly, and assess whether it is deserved or not. If not, they are much more adept at dismissing it than we are. All of this usually happens instinctively, with little recognition of the process.

Obviously I am speaking in generalities, which means there will always be exceptions to these findings. However, it is helpful to know about these generalities because many women have a great deal of difficulty understanding how men can be so "cold" or "uncaring," while men sometimes get nervous when a woman becomes "emotional" and "temperamental." In truth, men are not cold, unfeeling creatures as a rule; they simply are more prone to isolate their feelings. And women are not irrational and illogical creatures; we just take longer to get to the left-brain approach!

Understanding these typical male/female characteristics, we would be well advised to learn something from each other. Men would find it to their great benefit to be patient with our emotional responses and allow us time to make our way through them, for we will eventually—or at least most of the time—get to the logical and rational point. Furthermore, there are times when isolating one's feelings can hurt relationships and create misunderstandings.

We women, on the other hand, could reduce our stress levels a great deal by learning that there are times when feelings and emotions need to be isolated and set aside. This would enable us to detect false guilt before it completely swamps our emotions and carries us away.

Girlish Guilts

I often envision us women carrying our guilt backpacks with us all the time, collecting guilt as we go. These backpacks are stuffed full with what I call "girlish guilts," the small everyday guilts we accumulate without even noticing. These are the little nagging guilts that are peculiar to women; most men would never be bothered by these. They wouldn't know what we're talking about. Our sensitive natures make us more vulnerable to seeing things that are not there, reading between lines incorrectly, interpreting body language and facial expressions inaccurately.

Girlish guilts usually come in the form of saying "I'm sorry" and feeling responsible for events and situations that are not our fault. I'm not talking about expressing sympathy for something unfortunate, but feeling guilty and unconsciously taking blame that does not belong to us.

Here are some examples of girlish guilts to which a woman's first response will most likely be, "Oh, I'm so sorry!"

- A coworker says that while you were on vacation last week, the place fell apart and she had to work late every night. You feel guilty for having been gone on vacation.

- Your child says she got into trouble with her teacher because she left her homework at home, trying to shift the blame to you for not reminding her to take her homework to school. You feel guilty for not making sure your child took her homework.

- Your husband complains that the dry cleaners put too much starch in his shirt collars, looking at you as though you should have corrected the problem. You feel guilty for not noticing it before he did.

- Your sister says she tried to reach you three times yesterday and kept getting your voice mail. She didn't leave a message but still seems irritated that you were not there for her when she needed you. You feel like you've failed your sister.

- Your boss asks you where you put a certain file, and you are quite certain you have not touched that file, yet because he or she accuses you, you assume guilt.

- You report to your friend that you won't be able to attend the committee meeting on Saturday (which she belatedly called about) because of other family plans, and she comes close to frowning. You read her expression as a sign of disapproval, and feel obligated to keep explaining why you can't make it so she won't be mad at you.

- You promised to help decorate the church for an upcoming women's luncheon but then you come down with a bad cough and cold the night before. The tone in your friend's voice is anything but sympathetic when you call to say you can't make it, and you feel very guilty.

- Your mom says, "You mean you're not coming over for dinner on Sunday?" You have other important commitments—or maybe you just need some down time—and yet Mom expects you to visit every Sunday. You feel like you've ruined the day for her.

Are you getting the gist of these girlish guilts? These are not major issues of guilt, but they are significant enough to cause women to say, "If I'm accused, I must be guilty."

As I'm writing this, I'm thinking of a girlish guilt I have taken on just this week. In my clumsiness I fell on a city sidewalk a couple of weeks ago, and broke my fall with my left hand. At first I thought I would be okay, but later I realized I had more than just a bruise. I went to the doctor to have my hand checked, and he reported that I had a broken bone in my hand. This wasn't any big deal; it was merely a huge inconvenience accompanied by a little pain. I e-mailed my assistant at the church office where I serve as director of women's ministries and I casually mentioned that my e-mails would be short because I had broken my hand. Within a few hours flowers were arriving from the staff at church and e-mails and phone calls of sympathy came pouring in. Naturally I was very pleased that all these people cared, but immediately I felt guilty because I felt they were making too big a deal over a broken hand. I felt like only a person with a serious illness or who was near death should deserve this kind of attention, and I felt foolish for having reported my broken hand. Girlish guilt! I took it on unconsciously.

Unloading Girlish Guilts

Since most of us women carry this backpack of girlish guilts with us all the time, we need to find effective and appropriate ways to respond to such guilts. So let's take a look at each of these examples

I cited recently and identify better ways to respond to them. By using these specific examples of girlish guilts, I believe you will gain a better idea of how to respond to whatever girlish guilts you face. We have to learn to address these everyday guilts in different ways than we have in the past. We are breaking old, ingrained habits, habits of our mind, which may take some time to get over. And we begin by thinking, in advance, of more appropriate ways to respond to our girlish guilts.

Instead of saying "I'm sorry," here are some suggested responses that are more honest yet still kind. Each of these girlish guilts is false guilt, which means you have no need to apologize.

- *A coworker says that while you were on vacation last week, the place fell apart and she had to work late every night. You feel guilty for having just taken a vacation.*

   Proper Response: "I really appreciate all your extra effort. I'll do the same for you when you're on vacation."

- *Your child says she got into trouble with her teacher because she left her homework at home, trying to shift the blame to you for not reminding her to take her homework to school. You feel guilty for not making sure your child took her homework.*

   Proper Response: "Honey, a good idea would be to put your homework in your backpack the night before so you won't forget it."

- *Your husband complains that the dry cleaners put too much starch in his shirt collars, looking at you as though you should have corrected the problem. You feel guilty for not noticing it before he did.*

   Proper Response: "Maybe you need to try a different cleaners. You haven't been happy with them lately."

- *Your sister says she tried to reach you three times yesterday and kept getting your voice mail. She didn't leave a message but still seems irritated that you were not there for her when she needed you. You feel like you've failed your sister.*

Proper Response: "If I had known you needed to talk to me, I would have called you back right away."

- *Your boss asks you where you put a certain file, and you are quite certain you have not touched that file, yet because he or she accuses you, you assume guilt.*

  Proper Response: "Let me look through the files on your credenza and see if I can find it for you."

- *You report to your friend that you won't be able to attend the committee meeting on Saturday (which she belatedly called about) because of other family plans, and she comes close to frowning. You read her expression as a sign of disapproval, and feel obligated to keep explaining why you can't make it so she won't be mad at you.*

  Proper Response (ignoring the facial expression, which you may be misinterpreting anyway): "Do you know when the next meeting will be? If so, I'll put it on my calendar right now."

- *You promised to help decorate the church for an upcoming women's luncheon, but then you come down with a bad cough and headache the night before. The tone in your friend's voice is anything but sympathetic when you call to say you can't make it, and you feel very guilty.*

  Proper Response (ignoring the tone of voice, which you may be misinterpreting anyway): "Believe me, I'd rather be decorating with you than battling this cough."

- *Your mom calls and says, "You mean you're not coming over for dinner on Sunday?" You have other important commitments—or maybe you just need some down time—and yet Mom expects you to visit every Sunday. You feel like you've ruined the day for her.*

  Proper Response: "I love your cooking, Mom, but I just can't make it this Sunday."

You may be able to think of additional appropriate responses, but the principle here is that we need to break our bad habit of apologizing for things for which we are not guilty. Obviously, there's nothing wrong with saying the words, "I'm sorry." You could say,

"I'm sorry to hear you had a bad week while I was on vacation," meaning you empathize with your coworker's predicament without accepting the blame. Remember, you can empathize—that is, put yourself in someone else's shoes—without apologizing.

Refusing Undeserved Blame

It could be that you have allowed others to shift their blame to you for so long that you have become their dumping ground. Mothers, wives, and women do that far more easily and often than fathers, husbands, and men. That goes back to our nurturing natures, our desire to make everything right, and our tendency to feel guilty when accused without examining the facts. This is one place where we need to learn to isolate our emotional reactions and do some rational thinking.

Boundary-setting is essential in this process, and it needs to begin by surveying where we've fallen into this bad habit of accepting blame indiscriminately. We need to decide in advance where we will draw the boundaries and how we will communicate them to others (if indeed they need to be communicated). We women are not naturally very good at setting boundaries, so it will require some intentional effort on our part to make this happen.

Remember, if others are in the habit of using you as a dumping ground for their guilt, it's probably because you have allowed it to happen. True, there is guilt on the other side from those who are trying to put the blame on you, but you can still control your responses to their dumping efforts. Think of it as moths swarming toward a porch light on a summer night. When you turn that light on, they will come. But if you enclose the porch with screens, the moths will try to head for the light but be unable to get to it.

We need to build screens that prevent others from dumping guilt on us when we are not guilty. Or as my good friend Jan Silvious puts it, we need to imagine ourselves in a castle surrounded by a moat, and when people come our way to dump their guilt on us, we pull up the drawbridge so that they can't get to us. Let's look at some of the more common areas where we women tend to allow ourselves to be dumping grounds.

Mother Guilt

I am convinced that children are born with an instinct for manipulating their moms through guilt. They start doing this even before they learn to walk or talk.

If I cry loud and long enough, my mother will pick me up.

If I pout and look unhappy, my mother will give in.

If I say that all the other mothers do it, she will capitulate.

If I complain that I don't have what others have, my mother will buy it for me.

If I accuse my mother of not being there for me when I needed her, she will try to make it up to me with gifts or leniency.

Perhaps more than any other people in our lives, we moms cater to our children. It must be in the mom gene. But we are not doing our children any favors when we allow them to invade our boundaries and use us for dumping grounds. We have a responsibility to teach them to respect our boundaries and to accept responsibility for their own actions or inactions. We'll raise much healthier children when we do.

Begin with that toddler, teaching that you respond when he asks nicely, not when he throws a tantrum. Teach your pre-teens that whining and complaining are not accepted and don't work. Tell your teenager that your guidelines and principles are set by biblical standards, not by what all the other kids may be doing. Make it clear to your adult children that you are not responsible for their financial woes, and you won't be there to bail them out of their poor money management.

We set boundaries by our words and our actions. Words alone

are not always effective. But words followed by consistent action are effective at setting boundaries and making them stick. As you set these boundaries, you will be building the screen that keeps your kids from continuing to dump guilt on you.

Of course your children will test those boundaries, and if your resolve is weak, you'll end up caving in. Then the next time around, things will be worse than before. So be sure you are serious about following through on these boundaries. And be prepared for lots of badgering by your children, especially if they've been taking advantage of you for some time. They'll have a hard time believing you won't give in to their manipulative ways this time. Think of that screen you just erected, and keep that mental picture of those moths slamming into that screen every time they head for the porch light. Your kids may make repetitive attempts to get to you, but if you keep that screen up, keep repeating your boundaries, keep smiling, and keep assuring them you still love them but don't open that screen door, in the end, both you and your children will learn some valuable lessons and benefit from your boundaries.

Wife Guilt

I'm not married, so I'm no expert on this topic, but I know from my happily married friends that husbands can use their wives as a dumping ground for anything that may go wrong in the home or in money matters. Of course, marriage is a two-way street, so the dumping could certainly go in the other direction as well.

If you recognize areas in which you've been accepting blame from your husband that is not either wholly or partly yours, you need to have a good conversation with him, when you are not emotional and upset, and explain that it is to the benefit of your marriage for you to begin setting some boundaries about what is your fault and what is not. Give him some examples of what you mean:

- "Honey, every time you start paying bills, you accuse me of spending money foolishly. Most often when I explain where the money went, you realize that I didn't do anything wrong, but because you are frustrated, you still seem to want to blame me for our money problems. What can we do to work together better so that it's not you against me?"

- "Yesterday you blamed me because the dog had turned over the trash can and scattered trash all over the backyard. Do you really think that was fair?"

- "Last week your mother was upset because we didn't come over for Sunday dinner, and you blamed me for never wanting to go to your mom's. As you know, I always check with you when she invites us; it was your decision not to go because you wanted to watch the football game."

- "You're always blaming me for the condition of our son's room, yet when I insist that he clean it up, you say, 'Oh, don't bother him. He's a boy; boys never clean their rooms.' I'm determined that our son will learn to keep his room clean, and so I'm not going to clean it for him. I'd appreciate your help in this endeavor."

Instead of allowing instances like this to turn into fights and do damage to your marriage relationship, try to have a calm, rational conversation with your husband as you communicate your need for boundaries and your refusal to accept blame that is not yours. This must be done with the right words, the right tone, and most importantly, the right heart. If we speak the truth in love, as the Bible teaches (Ephesians 4:15), it can lead to understanding and clarification. But if we speak in anger or in an accusatory way, we will only make matters worse.

Authority Guilt

It is common for us to experience guilt feelings from those who are in positions of authority over us. Whether it is an employer, a pastor or group leader, a teacher or principal, or a parent or older sibling, we have a natural tendency to be easily intimidated by an authority figure. Even people who assume authority that is not rightly theirs can make us feel guilty before we know it!

Perhaps younger people have less of a struggle with this than those of us in the baby-boomer and beyond categories because in many ways they have been taught to challenge authorities and even to distrust them. But because we all have authority figures in our lives, we need to know what to watch for in case these people, because of their position, dump guilt on us—whether intentionally or unintentionally, deserved or undeserved. Here are some examples of authority guilt:

- *Workload guilt*—Feeling guilty because we didn't get enough work done
- *Unsatisfactory work guilt*—Feeling guilty because the quality of our work was unacceptable
- *Disobedience guilt*—Feeling guilty because we didn't follow instructions correctly
- *Unrealistic expectations guilt*—Feeling guilty because we were expected to accomplish more than we were able to do

If you recognize that you take on guilt from others far too readily, then you've made an important first step toward changing that bad habit.

Of course people in authority must confront genuinely unacceptable behavior or performance, but there are far too many instances in which those in authority dump their own guilt on those who report to them simply because they can. Earlier I cited an example about a boss who blamed his or her assistant for losing a file, but there are far more serious examples that can cause much harm, especially when that authority figure is a parent. How many young children have been seriously damaged by parents who blamed and punished them undeservedly?

I think we women are more susceptible to this authority guilt than men are for the very reason that we tend to feel things more deeply and we generally don't isolate our feelings very well. Furthermore, we have a deep desire and need to please people and to be affirmed, especially by those in authority over us, whereas men are typically more competitive and independent.

Again, our challenge is to set appropriate boundaries in our relationships with authority figures. In some cases we may find it necessary to put some space between us and them (when that is possible) in order to limit our exposure to their abusive tactics.

Setting boundaries is an important topic, and there is much good material written by Christian authors on the matter. Those who recognize that they have been allowing others to use them as dumping grounds for blame and guilt would be well advised to read more on this. If you recognize that you take on guilt from others far too readily, then you've made an important first step toward changing that bad habit.

Keep a Tender Heart

As we learn appropriate ways to deal with our girlish guilts, we don't want to lose the advantages we have as women. Having been a woman in a man's world through most of my career as well as my ministry, I am well aware of how easy it is to let the pendulum swing too far to the other side. I saw many women try to play like the boys, and try to use their tactics and mimic their behaviors. Not only is that a mistake, it is ineffective.

God created men and women with built-in differences, and when we women try to get "outside of ourselves," as the saying goes, we lose our most effective weapon—the femininity that God gave us. We don't have to lose our tender hearts, our compassionate tendencies, our sympathetic ears in order to get rid of girlish guilt. We certainly don't want to become so defensive that we can never say, "I'm sorry." We are women, and while we don't need to roar, we do need to treasure the special attributes that God gave us and use them wisely.

Use Your Own Slingshot

You remember the story of David, the shepherd boy, who volunteered to go up against the giant, Goliath (1 Samuel 17). King Saul was reluctant to let David do this, for he was only a boy and Goliath was a huge, experienced fighter. But David insisted and related to Saul his experience in killing a lion and a bear while he was tending sheep. He said, "The LORD who delivered me from the paw of the lion and the paw of the bear will deliver me from the hand of this Philistine" (verse 37).

So Saul relented, but then he tried to tell David how to kill Goliath. "Here," he said, "put on my armor, take my sword." David tried, but he immediately recognized that he couldn't use Saul's armor. "I cannot go in these," he said, "because I am not used to them" (verse 39). David took off the armor, went and found five smooth stones, and with his slingshot in his hand, he confronted Goliath. The first stone hit the giant in the right place and knocked him out. Then David cut off Goliath's head with his own sword and claimed victory.

How did David defeat Goliath? By using his own weapon, a slingshot. That's what he was good at; that's how he had defeated the lion and the bear; that's the gift God had given him. He had perfected his marksmanship as he tended his family's sheep day in and day out. If he had tried to defeat Goliath in Saul's armor, he would never have won.

Likewise, if we try to respond to girlish guilt—or anything else, for that matter—in ways that are unnatural to us, we will probably overreact and end up with more guilt.

I encourage you to become aware of your own girlish guilts. Listen to yourself respond when something goes wrong. Do you readily accept the blame, feeling that somehow, some way, you should have been able to resolve the problem? If you will begin to tackle these smaller guilts by changing your thought patterns and your verbal responses, you will be teaching yourself a most important principle in dealing with guilt. It is a matter of recognizing wrong thinking and substituting it with right thinking that will, in turn, help you to replace wrong responses with right ones.

Growing Free from Guilt

1. Which of these girlish guilts are you most likely to collect in a given day?

   ❐ I automatically say, "I'm sorry" far too often.

   ❐ One (or more) of my children knows exactly how to push my mom-guilt button.

   ❐ I accept blame at work from coworkers and management much too easily.

   ❐ My mother/father has a way of making me feel guilty even when it's not my fault.

   ❐ My mate tends to blame me for things around the house that go wrong.

   ❐ A leader in my church can make me feel guilty very easily.

   ❐ One particular friend tries to lay blame on me quite often.

2. Write some appropriate responses to the false guilts that are most frequent or bothersome:

   _____

   _____

   _____

   _____

   _____

   _____

3. In which of your relationships do you need to be more assertive about setting appropriate boundaries?

   ❐ With my children

   ❐ With my mate

   ❐ With my employer/manager

   ❐ With a leader in my church

   ❐ With one or both of my parents

   ❐ With a sibling or other family member

   ❐ Other

4. Write a script for a constructive confrontation with the person or people who exceed your boundaries most often or most flagrantly.

_____
_____
_____
_____
_____
_____
_____
_____
_____
_____
_____
_____
_____
_____
_____
_____
_____
_____
_____
_____
_____
_____
_____
_____
_____
_____
_____

5

Our Superwoman
Delusions

The dictionary says that a delusion is a "fixed, dominating or persistent false mental conception resistant to reason."[1] That's a pretty good description of many women today who are deluded in believing that they can and should do everything that needs to be done, never disappointing anyone, never missing a beat, and all without breaking a sweat. I confess that though I have recognized and talked about this tendency in women for years, I have never fully conquered that particular delusion myself, though I do believe I'm getting better at it.

Notice that a delusion is resistant to reason. In other words, we can know in our minds and with our logical, right-brain analysis that we cannot do it all and therefore we have to say no sometimes. But we refuse to say no because we've entertained this delusion for so many years that we must prove ourselves or our worth to others.

The problem with our superwoman delusions is that they make us prone to feelings of guilt because we are constantly confronting the reality that we really can't leap tall buildings in a single bounce! I think of a woman I knew in business some years ago who was very successful and hardworking and had risen very high in her company's hierarchy. At breakfast one day, as she was relating her impressive climb up the ladder to me, she told me what her next goal was and her timetable for reaching it. I remember talking with her about enjoying the place where she was, but it was clear that she wasn't able to do that. Each new step higher simply brought more self-imposed pressure on her part to do more, be more, earn more, achieve more. She had to prove that she could climb higher in that organization than any woman had ever done before, and as a result, she labored—literally—on a daily basis to prove she was superwoman.

Obviously, being goal-oriented and successful is a good thing, but when we are under the delusion that we must prove something to someone, and we are striving for new heights to establish our worth, then we open the door to the guilt that inevitably results when the ladder breaks or we discover there are no more rungs on the ladder, or that it was up against the wrong wall.

Is It Pride?

In confronting my superwoman delusions, I've had to admit that a great part of their origin is pride. My self-image has too long been dependent on my productivity—my ability to get a lot done in a short amount of time. I've basked in comments and compliments about my "many accomplishments." *How do you do it? I just don't know how you do all you do. You amaze me at all you get done.* Those kind of comments have fueled my superwoman tendencies and goaded me on to higher expectations of myself, because doing more would bring more commendations and affirmations, and then I'd feel even better about myself. I also didn't want to run the risk of disappointing anyone by not living up to my reputation!

You know, when you start to dig underneath some of your motivations and ask yourself why you do what you do, you usually find some pretty smelly stuff. I hope and pray that most of my work for the Lord has not been done for the praise of people and just to make me feel better about all that I do. Often, as I pray about my motivation, I simply say, "Lord, underneath all this mess is a woman who truly desires to please You and hear You say, 'Well done, good and faithful servant.' Please reveal my wrong motives to me and give me pure ones."

Jesus said, "I do not accept praise from men" (John 5:41). Many leaders in Jesus' day did not openly confess their faith in Him as Messiah because "they loved praise from men more than praise from God" (John 12:43). A good prayer that we need to pray frequently is that we will want God's praise more than the praise of people.

I'm convinced that none of our motives will be totally pure until we get rid of our fleshly human bodies and have our new resurrection bodies, which will be free from pride. One of heaven's greatest attractions for me is the knowledge that then I'll not have to fight against the human flesh any longer. Won't that be something!

Waking Up to Reality

When you need to be a superwoman in order to have good feelings about yourself, you're in for some brutal awakenings. Eventually you'll have to come face to face with the reality that you are not a superwoman, and you've been deceiving yourself all these years. So many women go into deep depression in the last half of their lives as they discover they can't do everything they used to do. The energy level goes down, the opportunities diminish, the body won't go as long and as hard as it used to, the younger women are on your heels ready to take over with their fresh ideas and energy, and suddenly you have to come face to face with the fact that you're no longer able to feel good through higher and better performance.

Too many of us are in bondage to the approval of others, and this takes us right into this superwoman pursuit. Are you there?

Superwoman Test

Here are some symptoms of the Superwoman Complex. Give yourself one point for each statement that describes you:

- ❏ I have a hard time saying no.
- ❏ I feel guilty when I don't accomplish everything that needs to get done.
- ❏ My to-do list never gets completed.
- ❏ I try to please everyone as much as I can.
- ❏ I think it's very important to keep a spotless house.
- ❏ I don't like to ask others to do the "dirty work," so I do it myself.
- ❏ I don't like to admit that I can't do something that's asked of me.
- ❏ I tend to overpromise and overcommit myself.
- ❏ There are many things I really want to do, which causes me to take on too many projects.
- ❏ My children, husband, coworkers, or boss run first to me when they need help with anything.

If you scored higher than five points in this nonscientific superwoman test, it is a good indication that you're facing the same struggle that many other women face—trying to jump through hoops and leap tall buildings and live up to unrealistic expectations. If you relate too well to these superwoman tendencies, no doubt you are also facing the aftermath of guilt that is inevitable as you fail to be all you think you should be.

Pray about the areas you checked and ask God for wisdom and discernment to help you overcome these superwoman tendencies.

Finding Balance in Our Lives

I never want to discourage women from reaching outside their comfort zones and discovering their potential in Christ. Far too many women are not willing to take any risks, and they settle for mediocrity. I am often disheartened when I think of all the things that could be done by talented and capable women who have never had a vision of what they could be, never even asked God to give them a vision.

Ephesians 2:10 is one of the most powerful verses in Scripture—it contains, in one verse, a life-mission statement for every Christian. This statement could hardly be clearer or more powerful:

> We are God's workmanship, created in Christ Jesus to do good works, which God prepared in advance for us to do.

I am awestruck each time I think that the God of all creation has a specific list of good works for me to do. How exciting is that? God has not called any of us to laziness or mediocrity. If we pursue the good works He prepared in advance for us to do, we'll be busy and we'll be tired and weary at times, and that's okay. Our problems with the superwoman syndrome begin when *we* are trying to do what we think we should do, rather than asking *God* to lead us to those good works He prepared for us. Any time we're "doing our own thing," we're headed for trouble. Anytime we allow someone besides God to set our agenda, we're headed for trouble. Anytime we live to please others rather than God, we're headed for trouble.

When we get outside of doing what God has put us here to do—outside of His will for our lives—we invite guilt to be our constant companion. That is because nothing can meet the deepest needs of our heart for satisfaction and fulfillment and significance except doing what God planned for us to do. And so, we often find ourselves in a catch-22, working harder and harder to please others and ourselves and gain affirmation and good self-esteem, only to discover that no amount of doing does the trick. The good feelings about ourselves and good self-esteem that we intuitively desire and need is found as a by-product of doing what God put us here to do—those good works He planned in advance.

I wonder how many godly women, women who truly want to please God, are on a treadmill of activity, taking on more and more responsibilities, accepting more unrealistic expectations from themselves and others, trying so hard to fit into that superwoman garb but never knowing the great joy of being where God wants them to be and doing what God wants them to do. I fear that there are too many of us saddled with our superwoman delusions, resisting the reasoning voice of God, and struggling with the guilt that comes when we learn we are not and cannot be superwomen. It's not in the list of good works God prepared for us to do.

At the end of His short earthly ministry Jesus could say to His Father, "I have brought you glory on earth by completing the work you gave me to do" (John 17:4). He had not healed everyone; He had not taught everyone; He had not converted everyone. Yet He could say, "I have completed the work My Father gave me to do."

Discover Your Good Works

Obviously, if we're going to do the good works God planned for us to do, we have to know what they are. Let me assure you that God doesn't send us on a treasure hunt to try to find His will. He is not playing hide-and-seek with us, teasing us with hints here and there, to see if we are adept at finding that seemingly illusive will of God for our lives.

The good works God has planned for each of His children will be, first and foremost, in complete agreement and harmony with God's Word and His principles as presented there. Hence, we need a good working knowledge of the Bible. That is imperative.

Second, the good works God has planned for us to do will make use of the gifts and abilities that God has placed in us. Hence, we each need to know how God has gifted us individually. If you've never studied the gifts that are listed in Romans 12:6-8, 1 Corinthians

12:8-10, and Ephesians 4:11, you would do
well to do so and discover which of those gifts
are evident in your life. Much good information
has been written on this topic and is readily available online or in your Christian bookstore. Two
resources I recommend are *What You Do Best in
the Body of Christ* by Bruce Bugbee (Zondervan,
2005), and *Living Empowered for Ministry* by Florence MacKenzie
(Scripture Union, 2002). (Florence's book can be obtained at www.
equippedforliving.com.)

> **God doesn't waste anything, not even our failures.**

Third, the good works God put us here to do will not come to
us in a strategic plan for our life, with every detail outlined and
every path clearly marked. God knows that plan, of course, but He
reveals it to us gradually as we grow in grace and our faith increases.
Knowing God's will should become a daily pursuit for us. If we seek
to know and do God's will today, and then again tomorrow, and the
next day, and the next—guess what? We'll be living in His will and
doing the good works He has planned for us to do.

You may be thinking, *Yes, but I've already missed God's will for
my life. I've already messed up. So, what do I do now?* Please know
that God is so creative, so incredibly efficient, and so gracious that
He has plans for us even after we've blown it. God doesn't waste
anything, not even our failures. I'm living proof of that. You've
already read my story in chapter 2 of how I willfully left God's will
for a ten-year period. I don't deserve to be used by God, but then
nobody does—so there you go!

If you really have no idea of what God has put you here to do,
begin by looking at your life today. Are you married? Do you have
children? If your answer is yes to either question, then you can
know that your job as a wife or mother is a very high priority with
God, and a good part of your "good works" will be involved with
those relationships and your responsibilities in them. Being a wife
or mother takes varying amounts of our time at different stages of
our lives, but they are always to be at the top of our list.

I've discovered that what God put me here to do is what I really love to do. God is a very intelligent manager of His human resources. He knows we work best when we enjoy what we do, so what He has gifted you to do will be something you will love doing. Oh, yes, you'll get tired and frustrated and weary at times, and parts of your responsibilities will be tedious and monotonous, but overall you will love doing the good works God put you here to do.

I can say with certainty that if your deepest desire is to know and do the good works God put you here to do, and if you search for that knowledge with all your heart, you will find it. My good friend Karen searched for two years to know what God put her here to do. She knew God had gifted her with a good mind, that she was very creative at working with her hands, and that she loved people. So for two years she prayed, "Lord, please give me something to do that uses my head, my hands, and my heart." She had no idea where God would take her, but she knew it would be meaningful and fulfilling.

After a short-term mission trip to a refugee camp in Namibia, Africa, which took her way out of her comfort zone, she knew God had put her here to help the women in that camp. She was able to share her vision with our church in such a powerful way that over the past six or seven years, she has organized and led a drive to help those people, mostly Angolans, in that refugee camp. We've built a church there and a woman's center, and we have delivered multiple truckloads of food and clothes and seeds and equipment. All of this was collected and arranged and organized by Karen.

When I went with Karen in the summer of 2005 to teach the Bible at the refugee camp, I witnessed how the women there loved her. After more than a dozen trips over there, she knew many of them by name, and they knew they had a friend in Karen. God continues to use her mind, her hands, and her heart to do the good work He put her here to do, and she has been transformed. She has had to overcome her great fear of public speaking, and it has not always been easy. She has had many heartaches and struggles along the way. But when you know you're doing what God put you here to do, somehow, by His grace, you just keep going.

Learn to Say, "It's Not My Job"

Does it make you angry when a store clerk or a customer service agent says, "It's not my job"? Those words do not make for good customer relations. But I'll never forget the day some years ago when I realized God had not called me to be a superwoman. It came to me when I was reading the twelfth chapter of Luke, where Jesus told someone, in essence, "It's not my job!" You probably never realized Jesus said that, but it's in Luke 12:13-14: "Someone in the crowd said to him, 'Teacher, tell my brother to divide the inheritance with me.' Jesus replied, 'Man, who appointed me a judge or an arbiter between you?' "

The man asked Jesus to be a judge, and Jesus basically said, "It's not my job." Jesus was healing people and casting out demons; it was obvious He had unusual authority. Apparently this man saw what Jesus was doing and decided He was the right person to settle this argument between him and his brother. But Jesus told him that He was not called to be an earthly judge, nor did He intend to try to become one. I'm sure Jesus was not unkind about this, but He certainly was direct. Jesus kept a single focus, and in the process, disappointed some people during His ministry here on earth.

In Mark 1:35-38 we see another occasion when Jesus disappointed some people:

> Very early in the morning, while it was still dark, Jesus got up, left the house and went off to a solitary place, where he prayed. Simon and his companions went to look for him, and when they found him, they exclaimed: "Everyone is looking for you!" " Jesus replied, "Let us go somewhere else—to the nearby villages—so I can preach there also. That is why I have come."

Can you picture this situation? The whole town had gathered to hear Jesus, and His disciples were most anxious for Him to come and please the crowd. I mean, preachers don't walk away from large audiences, do they? But Jesus knew what His priorities were and He made a decision to go elsewhere—undoubtedly disappointing His disciples and the crowd that had gathered.

I can't tell you how relieved I was to learn that there are times when it is okay to disappoint people. I had lived under the misconception that if I was everything I should be, everyone would be happy with me and I'd be able to please everyone. Now, that kind of thinking will lead you to burnout pretty fast. Are you living your life under that same misconception?

The old saying is so true—you can't please everybody. Jesus didn't; what makes us think we can? Furthermore, even well-intentioned people will try to tell you what they think you should do; like the disciples, they may have a set of expectations for you that are contrary to the priorities you believe are right for you. So, there will be times when even people close to you won't understand your refusal to fit into their plan.

Determining the right priorities for any given day and therefore knowing when we should say, "It's not my job" are dependent on how well we understand what are those good works God put us here to do. When we have a clear understanding of our biblical priorities and we seek to know God's will on a daily basis, God's Holy Spirit will give us clear inner guidance of when and how to say no. I've learned a lot about saying no by saying yes far too easily and then having to deal with the consequences of making a commitment before giving it careful thought and prayer.

Saying no to anyone is very difficult when we have put ourselves in the position of meeting the expectations of others. That's what happens when our worth as a person is based too much on what others think of us. When we are dependent on the opinions and affirmation of others in order to feel good about ourselves and what we're doing, then we are putting ourselves at their mercy. We're going to be continually jumping through their hoops, trying to be superwomen, in order to gain their approval and therefore feel we're okay.

Interestingly, the more we seek to know God's priorities for our lives and to understand and do the good works He put us here to do, the more we'll be pleasing to others. True, we won't please everyone, but our best hope of pleasing the most people is to please God first. No doubt the works He has for us to do will involve being a servant to others. We will stay involved in the lives of other people, but we will be doing so for the right reasons and in the right way. We won't be doing things for others in order to win their approval, which in turn will make us feel better about ourselves. We'll be serving others out of a pure motivation to do the good works God planned for us to do.

Appreciate the Seasons of Your Life

When you are young, you never imagine that you'll be anything but young. My self-image of myself has not aged one year, in spite of the reality that the calendar has advanced steadily and I am no longer young by the world's standards. I am having to learn to readjust my self-image to accept that years have passed and things do change.

There is a fine line to walk here, because I see far too many people who think themselves into being old, feeling old, and acting old! I refuse to fall into that pattern; I refuse to indulge in negative self-talk about getting old or feeling old. In a real sense, we truly are as old as we think we are, and I choose to think young!

Nevertheless, our bodies go through changes with time, our energy levels diminish, and even hard-driving Type-A personalities must recognize the need to change the pace a bit. (I prefer the phrase *change the pace* to the more-often used phrase *slow down*.) This change of pace can drive some women into depression because they are filled with guilt about not being able to do what they used to do.

Instead of regretting the change of pace in my own life, I'm trying to learn to appreciate it. I can now admit—without feeling guilty—that I don't want to work as hard and as long as I used to. That has taken some time. I can now rearrange my schedule so that I can enjoy a more leisurely morning, without those nagging guilt feelings that I should be at the office bright and early. I'm moving into a different season of life that has just as much value and opportunity and service as before, but at a different pace.

Recently I was talking with my friend Jan Silvious, and we were commenting on the reality that we are now the "wiser older women" whom the younger women look up to for help. It's a new self-image for us, and a little frightening at that. But it is encouraging to realize that the years of experience and work and learning that are behind us are indeed useful. We have "been there, done that" for so long that we do have some good wisdom to pass along. What a joy to be able to do that; what a great season of life!

Dump the Superwoman Delusions

I don't care what the dictionary says—we can get rid of the "fixed, dominating or persistent false mental conception resistant to reason" that we call the Superwoman Syndrome. It will take some effort, and we'll have to be intentional about it. But if you recognize that you've been caught in the trap of such superwoman delusions, I encourage you to identify them and then start praying about them. As a child of God, you have the Holy Spirit in you to empower you to have victory over those delusions. You'll be amazed how much freedom you will know once you overcome that resistance to reason and live in the reality that you are not superwoman. And the good news is that you don't have to be!

Growing Free from Guilt

1. Which of these superwoman wings do you need to clip?
   - ❏ I feel an exaggerated need to make everyone happy and meet everyone's expectations.
   - ❏ I find too much of my self-worth wrapped up in my abilities and productivity.
   - ❏ I take too much pride in proving I can do a lot of things.
   - ❏ I thrive on the praise and affirmation of people.
   - ❏ I find it very difficult to refuse people's requests, even when it's not my job to do what I've been asked.
   - ❏ I can't stand the thought of disappointing someone.
   - ❏ Other: _____

2. Do you feel you have a pretty good sense of what God put you here to do—the good works He planned for you to do?
   - ❏ Yes
   - ❏ No

     If yes, are you making those tasks the highest priority of your life?

     If no, what do you believe is keeping you from knowing God's will for your daily life?
   - ❏ Lack of Bible knowledge
   - ❏ Don't know what my spiritual gifts are
   - ❏ Never really asked God to show me what He put me here to do
   - ❏ Have felt that it's too late for me to do God's will
   - ❏ Have felt I'm not able to do anything for God at this stage of my life
   - ❏ Other: _____

3. Look at your responses to questions 1 and 2. What prayer must you lift up regularly in order to dump your superwoman delusions and get out from under your guilt? You might find it helpful to write your prayer:

   _____

   _____

6

Making
Comparisons

When I was a freshman in college, I came to the conclusion that something was wrong with my personality. My perception was that every woman should be quiet, reserved, and sweet. (Keep in mind this was before the days when women began entering the business world in a big way.) No doubt this was influenced by my Southern upbringing and my precious mother who was and is all those characteristics—and more.

I compared myself to the image of the ideal woman that was prevalent in my very closely knit evangelical Christian world, and felt very guilty that I did not measure up. I seriously wondered if my parents had brought the wrong baby home from the hospital, since I was so unlike my mother. Instead of quiet, reserved, and sweet, I was loud, up-front, opinionated, a take-charge risk-taker. No matter what group I was in, before I knew it, I was trying to be the leader and run the show.

My mother tells stories of how I badgered my older brother, Roger, and could talk him into doing my chores. She would tell me to do something, and in a few minutes she would see Roger doing what I was supposed to do.

As I grew older, I began to feel guilty for having this "aberrant" personality. I can still recall times when I was rebuffed by friends or teachers for being "out of line" in trying to take over. So I felt guilty about not being what a girl was supposed to be—a conclusion I reached by comparing myself to others—and made a decision to change my personality. Mind you, there were many aspects of my personality and behavior that needed polishing and refining, but I didn't understand it that way. I thought my whole personality was a mistake.

The summer after my freshman year in college offered me the perfect opportunity to make what I thought was this much-needed change. I was recruited to be a counselor at a Christian youth ranch several hundred miles from home, a place where I knew no one and no one knew me. As I took that long bus ride to the camp that summer, I decided to be a different person when I stepped off that bus. I pictured what I thought I should be—and it was another girl in my freshman class. I don't remember her name, but I can see her face even now. It glowed; she smiled all the time; everybody loved her; and she was quiet, reserved, and sweet. She could also sing like a bird—and I was a voice performance major. So, it was inevitable that she would become my role model. I could picture myself becoming her as I stepped off that bus with a completely transformed personality. And with a couple of months to spend at the ranch, I figured I'd have the change down pat by the time I returned to school.

I chuckle now as I recall this story, but I was dead serious about this at the time. And I tried so hard. I remember reminding myself to smile and to look sweet and not to talk so much. I had to think about it every minute because it wasn't me, but believe me, I tried.

I think my "makeover" lasted about two days—that's the best I could do. And instead of coming across as quiet, reserved, and sweet, I learned later that I was perceived as proud, conceited, and aloof. What a disappointment! I was stuck with myself, and it was years before I learned how wrong it is to compare myself to others and try to be somebody else. I carried that false guilt for 20 or more years, always believing that I needed to be like someone else but never being able to make it happen.

The Trap of Comparing

It's easy for us to fall into the trap of comparing ourselves to other people. We develop these tendencies early in life, and often others have taught us to do it. How many parents have said to a child, "Why can't you be like...?"? How many teachers have said to a student, "If you would do your homework like..."? When others are held up as role models and examples of the ideal child or student, girl or boy, man or woman, parent or worker, the trap door opens and we become vulnerable to comparing ourselves to others. When that happens, one of two sinful and opposite consequences usually results:

1. We begin to think we are better than others, or
2. We begin to think others are better than we are.

The Pride of Comparing

Consider that first consequence: thinking we're better than others. The parable of the Pharisee and the tax collector is appropriate here:

> To some who were confident of their own righteousness and looked down on everybody else, Jesus told this parable: "Two men went up to the temple to pray, one a Pharisee and the other a tax collector. The Pharisee stood up and prayed about himself: 'God I thank you that I am not like other men—robbers, evildoers, adulterers—or even like this tax collector. I fast twice a week and give a tenth of all I get.' But the tax collector stood at a distance. He would not even look up to heaven, but beat his breast and said, 'God have mercy on me, a sinner.' I tell you that this man, rather than the other, went home justified before God" (Luke 18:9-14).

We look at this Pharisee and think, "What an awful attitude!" Yet comparing ourselves to others can lead us into doing the very same thing. Whether it's comparing our outward appearance or our economic status, our educational accomplishments or our career success, our special gifts or our spiritual status, the sin of pride creeps in, giving us a false sense of security about who we are or what we have done.

Jesus said at the end of this parable, "Everyone who exalts himself will be humbled, and he who humbles himself will be exalted" (Luke 18:14). I remember some years ago when I asked God to teach me what it means to humble myself. How do you do it? Do you run yourself down a lot, refuse to accept compliments and hang your head and try to look humble? If humbling myself is what my Lord wants me to do, how do I do it?

The first lesson God taught me in humbling myself was to refrain from talking about myself so much. It caused me to realize how often in a conversation I was just waiting for an opportunity to tell something about me—usually something positive that would make me look good. I was chagrined to recognize this propensity, and shocked to see how clever I could be at bragging about myself without seeming to be proud or braggadocio. Learning to humble myself has been an ongoing and never-ending pursuit, but until I became intentional about it and literally asked God to show me how to do it, I never put into practice this Jesus-principle of humbling myself. I urge you to do the same. It is the cure for the prideful thoughts and attitudes that can result when we compare ourselves to others.

The Sin of Comparing

This second consequence that can result from comparing ourselves to others—thinking others are better than we are—is more insidious and deceptive. We don't recognize the sinfulness of this attitude because the arrogance and pride are not present. And it is this second result that can plunge us into the guilt syndrome. We need to recognize how wrong it is to fall into this trap of comparing ourselves to others and thinking negatively of ourselves.

Consider what Jesus said in the parable of the talents:

> It will be like a man going on a journey, who called his servants and entrusted his property to them. To one he gave five talents of money, to another two talents, and to another one talent, each according to his ability. Then he went on his journey. The man who had received the five talents went at once and put his money to work and gained five more. So also, the one with the two talents gained two more. But the man who had received the one talent went off, dug a hole in the ground and hid his master's money.

> After a long time the master of those servants returned and settled accounts with them. The man who had received the five talents brought the other five. "Master," he said, "you entrusted me with five talents. See, I have gained five more."

> His master replied, "Well done, good and faithful servant! You have been faithful with a few things; I will put you in charge of many things. Come and share your master's happiness!"

> The man with the two talents also came. "Master," he said, "you entrusted me with two talents; see, I have gained two more."

> His master replied, "Well done, good and faithful servant! You have been faithful with a few things; I will put you in charge of many things. Come and share your master's happiness!"

> Then the man who had received the one talent came. "Master," he said, "I knew that you are a hard man, harvesting where you have not sown and gathering where you have not scattered seed. So I was afraid and went

out and hid your talent in the ground. See, here is what belongs to you."

His master replied, "You wicked, lazy servant! So you knew that I harvest where I have not sown and gather where I have not scattered seed? Well then, you should have put my money on deposit with the bankers, so that when I returned I would have received it back with interest.

"Take the talent from him and give it to the one who has the ten talents. For everyone who has will be given more, and he will have an abundance. Whoever does not have, even what he has will be taken from him. And throw that worthless servant outside, into the darkness, where there will be weeping and gnashing of teeth" (Matthew 25:14-30).

Lessons About Comparing

Jesus gave us some extremely important principles in this parable, and for those of us who end up in guilt because we compare ourselves to others and find ourselves lacking, this parable unlocks some astonishing truth.

First, notice that the talents were distributed by the master "each according to his ability." And further, note that the master entrusted *his* property to them; these talents of money were the property of the master, not of the servants. Likewise, God has entrusted each of us with abilities and talents and with these come opportunities to multiply and gain more abilities and talents. God does not give each of us the same number of abilities or talents or opportunities. How and why He distributes them among us is His own design and purpose, and we may or may not understand it. Frankly, it's none of our business. And frankly, it doesn't matter how endowed one person may or may not be.

After His resurrection, Jesus taught Peter this same principle. In John 21:18-23 we find Peter comparing himself to John. Jesus had just told Peter about the kind of death he would die: "When you were younger you dressed yourself and went where you wanted; but when you are old you will stretch out your hands, and someone else will dress you and lead you where you do not want to go" (verse 18). Then Jesus said to Peter, "Follow me!" (verse 20).

Peter turned and saw John, and asked, "Lord, what about him?" (verse 21).

Jesus answered, "If I want him to remain alive until I return, what is that to you? You must follow me" (verse 22).

Peter wanted to be assured that John wasn't going to have it any easier than he was. He wanted Jesus to confirm that John would not receive preferential treatment, and Jesus basically responded to Peter that how He chose to use John was none of Peter's business.

I must confess that I have often wished God had given me talents and resources and opportunities that He has given to others. I have desired a different, more entertaining style of teaching and speaking. I have felt that the distribution of abilities and talents seemed inequitable. Some people are obviously more gifted than others, and our human reasoning tells us it is not fair. But I must learn—and relearn (as Peter did)—that how God has chosen to gift me versus how He has gifted others is simply of no consequence in the great scheme of things. What we have to recognize is that God is sovereign and He does as He pleases. It is His prerogative to lead each of us on whatever paths He chooses. What matters is my obedience to follow Jesus and be a good steward of what has been entrusted to me. If we could but learn this principle of simple obedience without comparing ourselves to others, we would save ourselves so much unnecessary stress and grief.

The second striking lesson we learn from the parable of the talents is that the reward for good stewardship is not based on quantity. This is in stark contrast to how we judge success in human terms. How many times have you won or lost based on quantity? The most runs wins the ball game; the most money buys the most things; the most sales wins the promotion; the most good grades wins the scholarship; and on and on we go through life, bombarded with evidence that the one with the most is the winner.

But Jesus turns this attitude on its ear with this parable. The man given five talents gets no greater reward than the man given two talents because both were equally faithful and equally successful in their stewardship. True, the bottom lines were quite different: one ended up with a total of ten talents while the other ended up with only four. But Jesus does not rate these servants as first place and second place, as we would do. He does not compare them with each other; rather, He compares what they achieved with where they began. Because they both doubled their talents, they were equally successful.

For us to break our natural tendency to compare the bottom lines, we need a paradigm shift of gigantic proportions. You have to pray this attitude into your life. Ask God to help you overcome your tendency to compare yourself to others who have more—more money, more accomplishments, more gifts, more education, and so on. That kind of comparing will keep you mired in guilt.

Third, the lesson we learn from the man with one talent is perhaps the most mind-boggling one of all. Instead of treating him with pity because he started with only one talent, the master treats him with what seems like cruelty as he condemns the servant for his poor stewardship.

Don't you find yourself feeling sorry for the man who began with only one talent? I can well imagine that his decision to hide it in the ground was prompted, at least in part, by comparing himself to the other two guys. Can't you hear him thinking, *Well, if I had five talents, I could surely do something, or even if I had one more talent, that would help. But I'm so far behind before I begin that there's no use trying. And knowing me, I'll just lose the one talent I have and end up with nothing!* Had you been the master to whom he must give an account, would you not have been tempted to let him off the hook?

Consequences of Comparing

Notice what happened to this third servant as a result of his comparing himself to those who had more:

- First, it made him fearful. He was afraid to lose the talent he had, since he compared and saw that he had only one. And that fear led him to a very irrational, unreasonable course of action. Knowing that the master was demanding and expected him to multiply his talents, he decided to dig a hole and hide it.

- Second, he became lazy. The master called him a lazy servant. When we compare ourselves to others who have more than we do, this will frequently happen. We lose our motivation and initiative and become lazy.

- Third, it led him into sin. The master identified him as wicked because he had failed to do what he knew he should do. In James 4:17 we read: "Anyone, then, who knows the good he ought to do and doesn't do it, sins."

- Fourth, he lost what he had. His worst fear was realized; the master took his one talent and gave it to the man with ten.

- Fifth, he lost his reward. Had he multiplied his one talent into two, he would have received the same reward as the others, and would have been given more. But he lost his reward because he compared himself to those who had more, decided there was nothing much he could do with what he had, became fearful and lazy, and lost all he had.

This servant's paralysis of mind caused him to do nothing, which may have increased his own self-perception that he was incapable of doing anything with the one talent and that he was likely to be a failure. He became his own worst enemy with this self-fulfilling prophecy that he couldn't do anything with what he had because what he had was so small and insignificant.

By his attitude and actions, this servant was basically saying to the master, "I wasn't treated fairly. I didn't have enough to begin with. It's not my fault that I don't have a success story to tell you, because you only gave me one talent to begin with."

Please think this through in your own life. Are you susceptible to these same kinds of thought patterns? Have you concluded that you are so lacking in some area(s) in basic skills and abilities—your share of the pie is so small—that you simply cannot contribute anything significant? That may not seem like a sinful attitude; it may even appear humble, but in reality, it is an accusation that God has not treated you fairly.

Comparing your bottom line to others who have more is as sinful as a prideful reaction when you think you are better than someone else. It's not as easy to detect, but it's there. Underneath the pity party is not only guilt, but a sinful belief that God did not create you the way you should have been created. It is a feeling that you could have done a better job than God in your design, and therefore it is a criticism of God's creativity in you.

Letting Go of Comparing

When I finally began to understand the sinfulness of my tendency to compare myself with others, it gave me a completely new perspective. Not only was I plunging myself into a lazy, nonproductive, shift-the-blame attitude, I was accusing God of unfair treatment. I was blaming God for my failure because He had not given me what I thought I needed to succeed.

It took me many years to believe that God's creativity in me was good and I didn't need to be anyone else. I was a long time coming to let go of my guilt that I didn't fit the mold I had created in my own mind of what a spiritual woman should be. I wasted far too many years thinking I had to be like someone else in order to please God and people.

What in the world is Jesus trying to teach us by such a drastic ending to the parable of the talents? I believe He is showing us the consequences of comparing ourselves to others who have more. It leads to ugly results. It destroys us. We lose what we have and end up in dark despair.

When I find myself falling into this pattern of thinking and comparing myself to others and wondering why I can't have things as easy as they do, I try to immediately remember what Jesus said to Peter, and I say to myself: *What is that to you, Mary? It's none of your business how God chooses to treat other people. Your job is simply to obey the Lord so that He will be glorified in your life.*

There is, once again, a fine line we walk here between our responsibility to realize all that God has created us to be, ever growing into the likeness of Jesus Christ, never satisfied to be "the way we are," and at the same time, appreciating and enjoying the way God has created us. When we continually compare ourselves to others, we open up the guilt gate and find ourselves mired again in that false guilt of feeling we don't measure up. And then we embark on that dead-end pursuit of trying to be who we were not created to be.

> **Accept the talents and gifts God has invested in you, and then set out to grow them as much as possible.**

So accept the talents and gifts God has invested in you, and then set out to cultivate them as much as possible. Do that by using them any way you can. Jump in the water and get wet. Often I'm asked how I began my radio ministry, which is now heard on over 500 radio stations internationally and reaches out in many other ways. Well, it began in my home in Chicago over 20 years ago as a Bible study for five or six women. That Bible study lasted several years, and to this day is one of the sweetest, best memories I have.

From that I started a small ministry at my church and became involved in other ministries there, serving in various ways. And much to my amazement, the doors continued to open for expanded outreach. But it all began where I was—in my home. And little by little God gave me opportunities to develop my gifts. I trust that a year or two or five from now, I'll be able to see even further growth in my gifts and talents but not because I'm supertalented. I am not. Rather any growth that takes place will be because God keeps His word. He has promised that when we are faithful with the gifts and talents we have, He will give us more.

There is wonderful good news in this parable, and we don't want to miss it. Jesus is teaching us that we will not be judged in comparison to others. Rather, we will be judged by where we started and where we ended. We have no control over how God created us, where He created us, and how we have been endowed with gifts and talents. That is God's responsibility. So it really doesn't matter whether we began with much or little. All that matters is how faithful we are to develop and multiply the gifts God has given us.

If you have been in the habit of comparing yourself to others and always ending up on the short end of the stick, you will be amazed by the freedom that awaits you when you finally stop comparing your bottom line with others, and concentrate instead on multiplying and improving the gifts and opportunities God has given you. I have found that as I've learned this lesson, not only am I more energized and motivated to be all that I can be, but I'm also set free to enjoy and appreciate others without comparisons, without jealousy, without envy.

That, my friend, is great freedom.

Growing Free from Guilt

1. Identify anyone you have habitually compared yourself to, whether it is a person you know, a role model you admire, or an ideal in your mind:

   _____

2. Identify the area(s) in your life that you compare to the person or persons named above:
   - ❏ Appearance
   - ❏ Size
   - ❏ Abilities or talents
   - ❏ Accomplishments
   - ❏ Family relationships (spouse/children)
   - ❏ Personality
   - ❏ Other: _____

3. When you indulge in these habitual comparisons, how does it affect you?
   - ❏ It discourages me.
   - ❏ It makes me feel unworthy.
   - ❏ It makes me jealous.
   - ❏ It causes me to want to give up.
   - ❏ It makes me feel I was not treated fairly or given a fair shake.
   - ❏ It causes me to work harder and try to be more like that person.
   - ❏ It makes me unhappy with myself.
   - ❏ Other: _____

4. Are any of the results you acknowledged in question 3 sinful? If so, are you willing to pray for deliverance from your tendency to compare yourself to others?

7

An Overly Active
Conscience

Did you ever think about the guilt that the apostle Paul must have struggled with after his remarkable conversion on the road to Damascus? I can imagine some sleepless nights for this great apostle—nights when he lay in bed remembering his persecution of the people who believed that Jesus was the Messiah. No doubt he had vivid memories of the day that Stephen was stoned to death for his faith in Jesus. During the stoning, Paul watched the clothes of those who killed Stephen and gave approval to what they were doing (Acts 7:54-60).

Paul's conscience must have bothered him at times even after he had been forgiven and called into ministry. Think of all the words he had spoken against Christ and His disciples; think of all the damage he had done to the new and brave believers in the early church; think of all the pain he had caused to so many people simply because they believed in Jesus. Those were blights on his conscience, and I doubt he simply forgot them all on that road to Damascus.

Among the clues to Paul's struggle are the many references he makes to conscience in his letters to the early church believers. There are 25 passages in the New Testament that mention or address the conscience, and the apostle Paul wrote all but six of them. And if you believe, as many do, that he wrote the epistle to the Hebrews, then all but two were written by him. He must have struggled with the guilt of his past, and his frequent references to having a clear conscience could indicate that this had not come easily.

The Need for a Conscience

Every person has a conscience, or at least had a conscience at one time. The dictionary says a conscience "is the sense of what is right and wrong in one's conduct or motives, impelling one toward right action."[2] Would that were always true—that everyone's conscience impels him or her toward right action. But we know that we can ignore our conscience, or corrupt our conscience so that it no longer performs this important function.

Paul wrote to Titus, "To the pure, all things are pure, but to those who are corrupted and do not believe, nothing is pure. In fact, both their minds and consciences are corrupted" (Titus 1:15). No doubt you know some people who no longer have a conscience that bothers them about anything because it has been corrupted through habitual neglect and sin.

Furthermore, our consciences are not necessarily foolproof guides. We can deceive ourselves or be deceived, or simply lack understanding. Paul also said, "My conscience is clear, but that does not make me innocent. It is the Lord who judges me" (1 Corinthians 4:4).

Paul said, "I strive always to keep my conscience clear before God and man" (Acts 24:16). That is good advice for all of us who are disciples of Jesus Christ. And his exhortation to Timothy was to hold "on to faith and a good conscience. Some have rejected these and so have shipwrecked their faith" (1 Timothy 1:19).

No question about it—we need to work at keeping our conscience clear and pure, which takes us back to our discussion in chapter 2 about confronting and dealing with true guilt. When we are quick to deal with that convicting voice of God's Spirit and keep a short account with the Lord, then we will keep a clear conscience that is free from that true guilt that comes when we are tolerating some area of disobedience in our lives.

An Overly Active Conscience

Problems arise, however, when you have an overly active conscience. Such a conscience is like a nagging person who badgers you and accuses you and hounds you night and day about actual or imagined failures or inadequacies. It's that inner voice that runs you into the ground with thoughts such as, *You can't possibly think you deserve that promotion, can you? You never do enough. Think of all you haven't done that you should have. Think of how much better she is than you are. You know how you failed the last time you tried to do that.* And on and on it goes.

This overly active conscience puts you behind the eight ball even before your day begins. No matter how much you do or how hard you try, it never is enough to still the nagging voice inside of you. An overly active conscience gives you a much-inflated sense of duty. You think you should do so much more than you really should do. It nags you until you are convinced that you never measure up to what is expected of you and therefore, you are driven to try to squash that nagging sense of inadequacy that your overly active conscience has imposed on you. But no matter what you do, you can never get rid of that nagging voice within—at least, not for long.

Unrealistic Expectations

An overly active conscience is susceptible to unrealistic expectations. These expectations come from various sources—from within ourselves, from parents (whether alive or not), from friends, bosses, co-workers, or even from a distorted understanding of God. It is fueled by our performance-driven culture, where good feelings and self-confidence are dependent on how well we perform and how much we do—whether or not we are able to live up to those unrealistic expectations.

This propensity to end up in bondage to unrealistic expectations comes from our need to have the approval of others. With an overly active conscience, a person can actually attract unrealistic expectations because she so desperately needs approval that she looks for ways to earn that approval by trying to do or be what is more than she can do or be. It becomes a vicious cycle of trying to live up to these expectations, failing to do so, setting the standards higher, feeling more guilty, and so on—all of which adds more fuel to the flame of that overly active conscience.

Satan loves guilt and wants to convince us that God could never love us again.

To an overly active conscience, ridden with unrealistic expectations, acceptance is always seen as conditional. The need to prove one's worthiness to others remains constant. While we should be concerned, to a point, about the feelings or expectations of others, an exaggerated concern for what others think will put you on the road to burnout, depression, and despair. An overly active conscience is a stern taskmaster who is only occasionally pacified and immediately requires that you prove your worthiness once again.

With her permission, I am quoting what my friend Beverley wrote to me about the guilt that kept her in bondage for several years:

> I guess it is so hard to write my thoughts about guilt because it is difficult for me to believe that God is so gracious as to forgive such grievous sins as I have committed. Instead, I hold onto my guilt like a badge of courage, or like a weight that somehow, if I carry it long enough, will sufficiently punish me for my sins and make me worthy in God's eyes. I forget that I am worthy in God's eyes only because He sees me through Christ. Even at my best I would still be unworthy to walk into the presence of the holy of holiest God.

Satan loves guilt and wants to convince us that God could never love us again. Maybe God loved us at one time, but not anymore. Why would He ever trust us and take another chance? Physical, emotional, and spiritual depravation are a result of Satan's attempts to pull this dark veil of guilt over our hearts.

That's what an overly active conscience will do to you—it will make you think you deserve to be punished in order to be worthy.

Your conscience tells you that you deserve punishment, and if God is not going to punish you, then you feel you must punish yourself. You assume that God will be pleased to see your self-inflicted punishment. To you, God's forgiveness is not enough.

Healthy versus Sick Consciences

A healthy conscience performs a needed function in our lives. It helps us to review what happened, how we responded, assess our culpability, and learn from our mistakes or failures. It sets up alarms and alerts in our brains to warn us of future mistakes. It triggers the review and rehearsal process that automatically occurs in our mind after something negative happens. It helps us strive toward keeping a clear conscience before God and man (as Paul stated in Acts 24:16). We all need healthy consciences, though it is not pleasant to deal with the guilt feelings they can produce. They force us to listen to the convicting voice of God's Spirit and make changes that are needed. They help us to be conformed to the image of Jesus Christ, which is the goal of every true believer.

When your conscience goes on autopilot, however, and never gives you a break; when that inner voice nags you night and day regardless of what you do; when you continually feel that something is wrong with you; then you are dealing with an unhealthy conscience. Not a corrupted or polluted one necessarily, but one that is destructive and that feeds messages that are lies and causes emotions that are debilitating.

I am coming to understand that anytime I am preoccupied with thoughts about myself, something is wrong. A servant of Jesus Christ who has a clear and healthy conscience and who seeks to please the Lord in all she does will have little time or desire to be self-focused. Thinking about yourself most of the time should be a red flag to any believer that your focus is probably not where it should be.

An overly active conscience will keep you self-focused. Unfortunately, contemporary society tells us to watch out for ourselves and, in many ways, encourages self-awareness. Much of the world's counsel, whether professional or otherwise, encourages us to be self-focused—so much so that it is unhealthy.

A biblical worldview leads us in the opposite direction. Every principle of Scripture teaches us to be God-focused and others-focused. Furthermore, the abundant life we all desire is ours only when we learn this paradoxical truth of Scripture: To die to yourself is to be alive unto Christ.

Finding Healing for a Sick Conscience

There is a passage in Isaiah 58 that has long spoken to me about what I need to do in order to find healing—healing for my heart, for my emotions, for my self-centeredness, for a sick conscience. Speaking to His wayward children, God says,

> Is not this the kind of fasting I have chosen: to loose the chains of injustice and untie the cords of the yoke, to set the oppressed free and break every yoke? Is it not to share your food with the hungry and to provide the poor wanderer with shelter—when you see the naked, to clothe him, and not to turn away from your own flesh and blood? Then your light will break forth like the dawn, and your healing will quickly appear; then your righteousness will go before you, and the glory of the LORD will be your rear guard. Then you will call, and the LORD will answer; you will cry for help, and he will say: Here am I (verses 6-9).

How do we find healing for a sick, overly active conscience? How do we live in the freedom for which Christ came to set us free? How do we really know the abundant life Jesus said is our birthright as children of God? One key essential is to get out of ourselves and stop being self-focused, whether it is a positive or negative view we have of ourselves. Either way, it keeps us mired *in* us, and that's the worse place to be!

We must ask God to give us a heart for others—to break our

heart with what breaks His heart, to lead us to those who need our help, and to show us the good works He has planned for us to do. Then our light will break forth. Then our healing will come quickly and we will produce works of righteousness.

For the ten long years that I walked away from my Lord and followed the path of my own heart, I was so self-focused that it makes me sick to think about it now. Everything was all about me, to the detriment of my role as a mother and daughter and friend, and definitely to the detriment of my testimony for Jesus Christ.

Once I returned to the Lord and began to follow His will for my life, I very quickly became involved in the lives of others. It wasn't that I sat down and mapped out a plan of how to be involved in helping others. It was simply the natural outcome of getting right with God. My desires changed and I wanted to use His gifting in me to His glory. That keeps you busy, I discovered, and before long there simply wasn't a lot of time for me to think about me. I was involved with others to the extent that by the time I put my head on the pillow at night I went to sleep, and when I woke up, my mind was filled with thoughts of others.

As this change took place in me, I wasn't all that aware of it. But one day, when I read these words in Isaiah 58, it dawned on me that my light was breaking forth and my healing was quickly appearing because I had become less self-focused. I'm sure most people learn this sooner and more easily than I did, but it was then that I came to the realization that trying to live in a world revolving around me was not only impossible, it was miserable!

Feeling Good About Yourself

Many people are in a desperate search to feel good about themselves, or to find that ever-illusive good self-esteem. When you think about it, that's what an overly active conscience is looking for— some measure of success that will quiet the nagging voice inside and convince you that you have worth and can feel good about yourself. But it's a useless pursuit destined for failure, because truly feeling good about yourself is a byproduct of investing your life in others and doing the good works that God put you here to do.

About 18 months after I relinquished control of my life back to God, I well remember walking down Wacker Drive in Chicago one beautiful spring day and looking around me and thinking about how beautiful the world was. Suddenly it dawned on me—I was happy! But how could I be happy when my circumstances had not changed? For ten long years I had thought my circumstances had to change before I could be happy. Then I recognized how wrong I had been. Here I was feeling good about myself exactly the way I was and where I was.

The longer I have lived in harmony with God's will for me, the more I have come to understand that feeling good about myself can be realized only when it is no longer the goal of my life nor my life's pursuit. Feeling good about myself will always be dependent on knowing that I am walking in His way (faltering as it may be at times), striving to keep my conscience clear before God and man, and basking in His never-failing, all-encompassing grace and love.

Understanding God's Grace

How many songs do you know about grace? How many sermons have you heard about grace? No doubt you've seen the acrostic that attempts to define grace as

God's
Riches
At
Christ's
Expense

C.S. Lewis, when asked to identify the one thing about Christianity that set it apart from all other religious, responded, "Oh, that's easy. It's grace." No other religion offers God's love and redemption coming to us free of charge, as a gift, with no strings attached, no performance required, no standards to meet. Only Christianity dares to make God's love unconditional.

Appreciating the Word *Grace*

Grace is a word that we use in many different ways. In his book *What's So Amazing About Grace?* Philip Yancey calls it "the last best word."[3] Some words get worn out through use, and over time we find it necessary to substitute other words that better convey our meaning.

For example, at one time the word *charity* meant the highest form of love. But today, *charity* has a totally different meaning to us. That's why the word translated "charity" in the King James version is translated differently in more modern versions of the Bible. In fact, most people would say, "I don't want your charity" as though the word were pejorative.

But the word *grace* has survived through the ages without losing its punch, without becoming stale or worn out. For example, the song "Amazing Grace" is sung all over the world by people who have no understanding of or who don't believe in its message of salvation through Jesus. But the idea of grace appeals to everyone. Somehow instinctively we recognize that we want grace, we need grace, we yearn for grace.

Living in Grace

The sad truth, however, is that many of us never live in that wonderful grace even after we've received it, even though we believe it and sing songs about it. Our daily experience often does not reflect that we have been given this amazing grace. We live grace-less lives because we are under the burden of an overly active conscience that keeps us from joy and peace and freedom.

I've often lamented that I have never been a graceful person. I can trip over my own two feet without any reason. I bump into chairs and desks and trip over rugs and steps far more than the average person. I'm not graceful by those standards, but I'm so thankful to know that I can be a grace-full person—one who is full of God's grace. And as I come to a deeper understanding of God's grace to me and I see again and again that it is lavished upon me in spite of my total unworthiness, then I can fill my mind with this truth, which eventually drowns out that nagging voice within me that is fueled by an overly active conscience.

Living in grace is my escape from the plague of an overly active conscience. You have to work at it some days; you have to retrain your thought patterns frequently. But this is ours in Christ, and we should not settle for anything less.

Growing Free from Guilt

1. Do you recognize within you any symptoms of an overly active conscience? If several of the following symptoms are descriptive of you, it could be an indication you're dealing with an overly active conscience.

   ❏ As soon as my days begin, I am bombarded with thoughts of worthlessness or inadequacy.

   ❏ Rarely a day goes by that I do not accuse or blame myself for some failure.

   ❏ I have very high expectations for myself that I rarely achieve.

   ❏ Even after I've had some success, I find fault with myself and feel I should have done more.

   ❏ I feel guilty if I don't feel guilty.

   ❏ My thoughts about myself are mostly negative.

   ❏ I think about myself in negative ways most of the day.

2. Are you actively involved in the lives of other people—that is, more than just your typical family duties and responsibilities?

   ❏ Yes

   ❏ No

   If not, do you think you need to reach out more to others? What are some ways you can do that?

   _____

   _____

   _____

3. How often in a given day do you consciously meditate, if even only for a brief moment, on how good God has been to you and the richness of His grace to you? What are some ways He has shown you His goodness and grace?

   _____

   _____

   _____

8

Believing Wrong
Messages

As the director of women's ministries in my church, I frequently have the privilege of listening to women and trying to disciple them in their faith walk. What I hear so often are stories of women dealing with guilt that comes from believing wrong messages. Sometimes these wrong messages or lies have been programmed into their minds through other people. Other times these wrong messages come from their own errant thought processes and their lack of understanding the freedom they have in Christ.

One single mother lamented over the two divorces in her life and saw herself as permanently soiled and damaged goods because of these broken relationships. Both divorces had occurred before she was aware of what it meant to be a Christian, and before she had made her choice to accept Jesus. As we worked through some of the baggage she was dealing with, I said to her, "You are no longer condemned. God sees you as pure and white because you now have the righteousness of Jesus Christ."

Her eyes welled with tears. "I just can't believe that God sees me as white and pure," she said. She knew she was forgiven of all her past sins; she understood that the past would not be held against her ever again. But she had seen herself as impure and messed-up for so long that it was difficult for her to believe that God saw her differently.

Another dear friend, Lucille, who has gone on to be with the

Lord and left us far too soon due to cancer, was such a great joy to know because she seemed to grasp her worth in Christ early in her faith walk, and she was quick to throw off the wrong messages she had believed all her life.

Lucille was the last of four or five children, and she was not a planned child. Though she was well cared for and lived in a fairly affluent home, her mother had damaged Lucille's self-image greatly during her years at home. Lucille said hardly a day went by that her mother didn't comment on the fact that Lucille was unexpected, unwanted, and her birth and presence in the family caused her mother great hardship. Some children would have responded through rebellion, but Lucille responded by trying to make herself so good and do so well in everything she did that her mother would finally admit that she was not an accident or a burden. Those words of affirmation never came.

As an adult, Lucille excelled in every area of her life, and her career was promising and successful. Moving away from her mother's daily influence, Lucille developed a tough exterior and made up her mind that no one would hurt her again. Her family had been religious in some ways, attending church regularly, but Lucille quickly abandoned that practice, deciding that God had not done well by her. She also never got past the messages that her mother had programmed into her mind, and she never felt loved or worthy in spite of her track record of success.

When Lucille was in her early fifties she was invited to visit our church by a persistent friend who simply wouldn't take no for an answer. When she did, she heard about a God she was totally unfamiliar with—a God who loved her. She kept coming, and many of us became her friends. One New Year's Day, several of us gathered at my home for food and fellowship and she listened to us talk about how Christ had changed our lives. She made her decision that day to make Him Lord of her life.

From that day on, Lucille glowed. She immediately got it—God loved her, she was worthy, she was valuable because God loved her.

And she was able to erase those wrong messages that had plagued her for so long. Time and again she would say to me, "I just can't get over how much God loves me." She never lost her wonder over God's forgiveness, and she was able to put the past behind her more quickly and completely than most anyone else I've ever known. She simply focused on the truths that God had loved her from before she was born, He had planned all her days, she was His child, and she was valued. She replaced the wrong messages with the right ones, and lived her remaining five or six years in the glow of God's love.

The Source of Wrong Messages

What wrong messages have you believed that have caused you to feel guilty? Here are some of the more common ones:

Wrong messages from others:
- Overbearing parents have often fed their children wrong messages by telling them they are not meeting their expectations.
- Critical mates can cause lots of guilt by their constant reminders that things have not been done well.
- Bosses or managers can send messages of inadequacy and incompetence by their never-satisfied demands.
- Anyone in a position of authority or perceived authority can send negative messages about our performance or worthiness—messages we tend to take seriously.

Wrong messages from our culture:
- The image of the ideal woman as extremely thin and ageless causes many women to carry constant guilt because of their size or appearance.
- The "you-can-have-it-all" message portrayed by successful women in the limelight drives many of us to try to be superwomen, resulting in feelings of guilt when we fail.

Wrong messages from the past:

- Any failures from your past have the potential of keeping you mired in the belief that you will always be a failure.

- Rejections from your past can cause you to believe you are unworthy of acceptance and love.

- A dysfunctional family life from your childhood—that is, divorced parents, abusive relationships in the family, one-parent home—can lead you to believe that you caused or contributed to the dysfunction, resulting in a load of false guilt.

You may be able to add some additional wrong messages you have believed and still do believe. Merely recognizing how inaccurate they are is not enough to overcome them, and some are so deeply embedded that the passage of time does not seem to heal or change them.

Erasing Wrong Messages

When I record my radio programs, I have the luxury of erasing any bobble I make and re-recording it so that when the program airs, no one hears my mistakes. It might appear as though I never make one! How we wish we could do the same thing with our minds—simply obliterate the mistakes and never again have to confront them. However, only God has the ability to erase His memory, as we read in Isaiah 43:25: "I, even I, am he who blots out your transgressions, for my own sake, and remembers your sins no more."

My guess is that if you are a believer in Jesus Christ, born from above, you have been taught this truth—that when God forgives your sins, He remembers them no more. We talk it and sing it and quote it, but learning to live in it is another story.

I doubt any of us can ever totally erase the memories of our sins, even though they are forgiven. And it is equally difficult to erase wrong messages that have been ingrained in our minds for a long time. We seem to be able to remember what we should forget and forget what we should remember!

I can still remember the words spoken to me by a camp administrator when I was a sophomore in high school—words of condemnation for my behavior, words that came as a complete surprise to me, words spoken in a meeting of all the camp personnel. What a silly thing to keep stored in my limited memory bank, but there it is. And if I choose to, I can bring that memory up again and relive the same horrible feelings of unworthiness and disgrace that I felt at that moment. If that comparatively insignificant event is still vivid in my mind, how much more vivid are the more significant messages many of us carry with us, and how much more difficult it is to erase them!

All through our lives we collect memories of past sins, words of condemnation spoken by those in authority over us, the feelings of worthlessness caused by our failures, and more, and we find ourselves remembering them and feeling guilt and shame for years to come. Oh, for some magic delete button to purge them away forever!

That button does not exist, but there is an answer. And once again, we must go back to a basic principle of Christian living which few of us have ever learned or applied. In my book *What Would Jesus Think?* I cover this in detail, but I find that on any topic this principle must be restated, for indeed, most of our struggles take place in our thought patterns and what we allow ourselves to dwell on. Therefore, the answer must take place in our minds as well.

Paul addressed this struggle in his second letter to the Corinthian Christians, in which he taught them how to fight their spiritual battles:

> Though we live in the world, we do not wage war as the world does. The weapons we fight with are not the weapons of the world. On the contrary, they have divine power to demolish strongholds. We demolish arguments and every pretension that sets itself up against the

knowledge of God, and we take captive every thought to make it obedient to Christ (10:3-5).

I find that one of the most difficult concepts of our Christian journey to communicate is the balance between what Christ has done for us and what we are called to do. Christ has redeemed us and forgiven us not based on our performance but solely on His work of redemption by His death on the cross, His burial, and His resurrection. No amount of good works on our part could ever gain this position we have as sons and daughters of God. It is God Himself who has "raised us up with Christ and seated us with him in the heavenly realms in Christ Jesus" (Ephesians 2:6). We have been given a free gift from the heart of a merciful and gracious God, and this gift was made possible because Jesus paid the debt for our sins.

So while performance is never a part of our salvation, still certain disciplines and duties are necessary after we are born from above so that we can grow in the grace of Jesus Christ and be transformed into His likeness with ever increasing glory (2 Corinthians 3:18). Bringing our thoughts into captivity is one example of what we must do in order to live in the freedom that Jesus purchased for us. This freedom is our birthright as children born into the family of God.

Imagine that you were born into a family of great wealth and you were given a bank account of considerable size that was readily available to you. No matter how great the sum of money, it is useless to you unless and until you write a check and take some of the cash for your own benefit. It's not a perfect analogy, but in a sense the same is true of our Christian journey. Because we are born into God's family, we have the resources we need to transform our thought patterns, but we have to write the checks that release those resources.

The Fail-Proof Delete Button

I said there was no magic delete button we can use to erase the wrong messages in our memories, but there is a fail-proof method we can turn to for help. Frankly, I am a bit skeptical of anyone who claims to have any kind of formula for success in the Christian life. For sure, we all have unique relationships with our heavenly Father and He deals with each of us in ways that are tailored to our specific needs. As the Master Teacher, He knows the learning methods that work best for us and guides us "in paths of righteousness for his name's sake" (Psalm 23:3). I've learned that others don't have to march in my spiritual parade and take the same path I do in their faith walk. God is infinitely creative and He doesn't make cookie-cutter Christians!

But there are some principles of the Christian life that are eternally true and that will benefit every Christian who applies them to his or her life. So, I share this fail-proof method in full confidence that it is so firmly rooted in the truth of God's Word that everyone and anyone can and will be blessed by it.

Taking Your Thoughts Captive

To erase wrong messages that plague you with guilt and keep you mired in lies, you must bring every such thought into captivity and force it to be obedient to Christ. That is your part in this process. You must recognize the wrong thought pattern and then, by a specific choice and decision on your part, learn to erase the thought pattern that is giving you those wrong messages by replacing it with right thoughts.

When you become truly tired of losing this mental battle and being continually defeated by the wrong messages that keep replaying in your mind; when you desire more than anything else to change those thought patterns in order to please the Lord Jesus and be more effective in His service; when you are willing to do the mental discipline that is necessary in order to erase these wrong messages, then you are ready for God to empower you to do what you can never do on your own.

Here again is that balancing act between what Christ has done and what we must do. Changing your thought patterns is beyond your capability; simply gritting your teeth and determining to do better is not enough. Philippians 4:13 says, "I can do everything through him who gives me strength." You and I must set our will to bring every thought into captivity and make it obedient to Christ. But that is done "through him who gives [us] strength." We turn on the switch; He supplies the power. We write the check; He provides the money in the account.

Replacing Wrong Messages with God's Truth

Setting our will to do our part begins when we want it, and when we ask for His power in us to do it. Next comes the fail-proof method. The way to effectively get rid of wrong messages that keep you in bondage is through Scripture memorization. You memorize portions of Scripture that directly address your particular wrong messages, and when a wrong message begins to replay in your mind, you immediately begin to recite the Scripture that counters that wrong message with God's truth.

> **Are you bombarded with wrong messages from other people...? Delight in God's Word.**

Jesus said "If you hold to my teaching, you are really my disciples. Then you will know the truth, and the truth will set you free" (John 8:31-32). How do you "hold to" a teaching? When you were in school and you needed to "hold to" a teaching so you could pass a test, what did you do? You rehearsed it over and over again until it was firmly established in your mind and you could therefore remember it easily and correctly.

When you memorize Scripture, you have to go over it many times, and the process of doing that helps to reprogram your mind. Then when wrong messages begin to invade your thought life, you can call upon that truth stored in your memory bank and use it to replace the wrong messages. You simply begin to quote the truths that will set you free. That, I promise, is a fail-proof method.

The longest chapter in the Bible is Psalm 119, and all but two of the 176 verses in that chapter refer to the importance and power of Scripture. Consider this portion:

Though the arrogant have smeared me with lies, I keep your precepts with all my heart. Their hearts are callous and unfeeling, but I delight in your law. It was good for me to be afflicted so that I might learn your decrees. The law from your mouth is more precious to me than thousands of pieces of silver and gold (verses 69-72).

Are you bombarded with wrong messages from other people—lies that have been smeared in your mind for years? Delight in God's Word. Memorize Psalm 119:69-72 and begin the process of erasing other people's wrong messages with God's truth. You can even thank God for the wrong messages which have caused you to learn His decrees; you can say with the psalmist, "It was good for me to be afflicted" with these wrong messages, because they have driven me to know and love His Word, which is more precious than silver or gold.

Here is another great truth from Psalm 119:

I gain understanding from your precepts; therefore I hate every wrong path. Your word is a lamp to my feet and a light for my path. I have taken an oath and confirmed it, that I will follow your righteous laws. I have suffered much; preserve my life, O Lord, according to your word (verses 104-107).

Have you suffered much from wrong messages others have taught you, or from our culture, or from your past? Your life can be preserved and you can be set free from those wrong messages by the Word of God.

I am absolutely convinced that anyone who is willing to do this will find healing and freedom. I have spoken at a specific women's retreat in Nashville, Tennessee three times over the past ten years, and on my last visit, Dolly, one of the women who has been a part of the leadership of this retreat since its beginning stopped me and said, "You just don't know how you changed my life." Well, I couldn't imagine what I had said that would change her life. I had a hard time even recalling what my topic was when I spoke there previously, so how could she remember anything I had said?

Dolly went on to explain that I had challenged the women to memorize Psalm 139. She had taken the challenge, and that had changed her life. She told me how God has used that Scripture time and again to change her thinking, to reprogram her mind, and to deliver her from wrong messages that had kept her in bondage for years.

It wasn't my great words of wisdom that changed Dolly's life. It wasn't my ability to speak with "the tongues of men and of angels" (1 Corinthians 13:1) that transformed her. It wasn't the fascinating stories I told or the tear-jerking messages I gave. It was God's Word, memorized and placed into her mind, for use by God's Spirit to empower her to change thought patterns and set her free.

I then remembered that my challenge was not a part of my prepared message. It was an "add-on" that came to my mind as I was speaking. I had thought about my Sunday class of women at my church, who had memorized Psalm 139 together and quoted it together. Each Sunday as we were in the process of memorizing the verses, we would hear testimonies of how God was using certain portions of His truth to set women free from wrong thinking. Interestingly Psalm 139 spoke to many varying needs. God's Spirit applied it in unique ways to the individuals who memorized the chapter.

As Dolly told me her story, I thought to myself, *Why am I reluctant to suggest Scripture memorization to people?* I suppose it's because I can almost hear the groans when this path to freedom is presented. I know all the excuses: I'm too old to memorize anymore. I just can't memorize things. I never was good at memorization. It's just too hard for me to do. And I also know how inconsistent I have been in my own attempts to memorize Scripture. I seem to run hot and cold on it.

Recognizing the Power of Scripture

The reason Scripture memorization is so helpful is not because you actually remember the verse perfectly. Rather, it is the *process* you go through to get there—the many times you must repeat and repeat and repeat that passage in order to memorize it. That is where the benefit lies. Each time you repeat the passage, you are reprogramming your mind with truth that will set you free.

My class and I memorized Psalm 139 a few years ago, and later on we memorized Psalm 103 together. I probably wouldn't be able to recite them letter-perfect at this moment, but I surely do know the content of those psalms. And with very little effort, I could bring them back to a quotable stage. They are engraved in my mind and my heart. When I hear any part of those chapters quoted in a sermon, I know exactly what it says and where it is. That is true of every portion of Scripture I have memorized even from my youth. You see, God's Word is eternal: "The grass withers and the flowers fall, but the word of our God stands forever" (Isaiah 40:8).

My mom memorized Scripture consistently. She signed up for a Bible memory course and learned large portions of the Bible, which she had to quote regularly to her accountability partner—and the recitations had to be letter-perfect. In addition, she memorized some books of the Bible as she taught those books to her Sunday women's class.

She is now 94 years old as I write this chapter, and dementia is taking its toll on her memory. She has trouble remembering the answer to a question she asked you less than one minute before; she can't recall what she ate for breakfast or even if she ate breakfast. It has been heartbreaking to watch her lose her memory and her ability to hold conversations given her previous mental acuity. Because of her dementia I never thought she would be able to remember the scriptures she memorized; I just assumed that she had lost her memory of Bible verses as well.

One beautiful spring day as I was pushing her outside in her wheelchair, I simply said, "This is the day the Lord has made." Without a moment's hesitation she completed the verse for me: "We will rejoice and be glad in it." I was surprised that she could remember it. So, I started another verse, and she completed it. I started Psalm 23, and she completed it. I sat down with her on that beautiful day and started as many passages as I could recall in the King James version text, and without fail she could finish them.

I hurriedly went to a phone to tell my brother about it, and he was as surprised as I was. We siblings had all assumed that the memory loss our mother was experiencing would take its toll on the scriptures she had memorized. But I'm here to tell you that the Word of God abides forever. Though I cannot explain it, it seems there is something special about memorizing God's Word. Many people have told me stories of elderly relatives—including some with Alzheimer's—who can no longer recognize people or put a coherent sentence together yet they can quote the scriptures they memorized years before.

So, I am wholeheartedly recommending that you memorize Scripture to help you erase those wrong messages. God's truth will set you free. It is a promise from our Lord Jesus Christ and it is fail-proof. To help you, I have listed some passages of Scripture that counteract the common wrong messages many struggle with. But whether you memorize one of these passages or find one more appropriate for you, if you really want to be set free from the wrong messages in your mind, this will work. Remember, step one is to determine whether or not you want to be set free. You have to be willing to do your part. And you can be absolutely assured that God will do His.

Growing Free from Guilt
God's Cure for Wrong Messages

Wrong Message	Scriptural Antidote
My past sins are too great.	*Psalm 103:8-12:* "The Lord is compassionate and gracious, slow to anger, abounding in love. He will not always accuse, nor will he harbor his anger forever; he does not treat us as our sins deserve or repay us according to our iniquities. For as high as the heavens are above the earth, so great is his love for those who fear him; as far as the east is from the west, so far has he removed our transgressions from us."

Isaiah 43:25: "I, even I, am he who blots out your transgressions, for my own sake, and remembers your sins no more." |
| I am not very smart or talented. | *Psalm 139:13-14:* "You created my inmost being; you knit me together in my mother's womb. I praise you because I am fearfully and wonderfully made; your works are wonderful, I know that full well."

Matthew 25:23 (from the parable of the talents): "His master replied, 'Well done, good and faithful servant! You have been faithful with a few things; I will put you in charge of many things. Come and share your master's happiness!'" |

I've messed up too much, too often.

Philippians 3:13-14: "I do not consider myself yet to have taken hold of it But one thing I do: Forgetting what is behind and straining toward what is ahead, I press on toward the goal to win the prize for which God has called me heavenward in Christ Jesus."

Isaiah 43:18-19: "Forget the former things; do not dwell on the past. See, I am doing a new thing! Now it springs up; do you not perceive it? I am making a way in the desert and streams in the wasteland."

Isaiah 61:1-3: "The Spirit of the Sovereign LORD is on me, because the LORD has anointed me to preach good news to the poor. He has sent me to bind up the brokenhearted, to proclaim freedom for the captives and release from darkness for the prisoners, to proclaim the year of the LORD'S favor and the day of vengeance of our God, to comfort all who mourn, and provide for those who grieve in Zion—to bestow on them a crown of beauty instead of ashes, the oil of gladness instead of mourning, and a garment of praise instead of a spirit of despair. They will be called oaks of righteousness, a planting of the LORD for the display of his splendor."

I can never do anything for the Lord.	*Philippians 4:13:* "I can do everything through him who gives me strength." *1 Thessalonians 5:24:* "The one who calls you is faithful and he will do it."
I don't have the right looks or personality.	*1 Samuel 16:7:* "But the LORD said to Samuel, 'Do not consider his appearance or his height, for I have rejected him. The LORD does not look at the things man looks at. Man looks at the outward appearance, but the Lord looks at the heart.'" *1 Corinthians 1:26-29:* "Think of what you were when you were called. Not many of you were wise by human standards; not many were influential; not many were of noble birth. But God chose the foolish things of the world to shame the wise; God chose the weak things of the world to shame the strong. He chose the lowly things of this world and the despised things—and the things that are not—to nullify the things that are, so that no one may boast before him."

9
Accepting
Condemnation

Early in the life of my radio ministry, I learned a valuable lesson about condemnation. I invited a person into my life who needed love and acceptance because of baggage from her childhood and a broken marriage. I sincerely but mistakenly thought that associating with me could help her find healing and give her the support she needed to put the past behind her and move on.

For the time we were associated, I labored under the assumption that my presence in her life would be beneficial to her, and though it was at some sacrifice of my own, I stayed with the plan because I thought I was doing something good. But slowly, subtly, she began to condemn me. I did not recognize it; I could not have verbalized it at the time, but little by little I found myself guilt-ridden because of her condemnation.

What did she condemn me for? Nothing specific. It wasn't that she confronted me or challenged me about anything in my life. It was just a slow dark blanket that descended upon me anytime she was around, and an abiding feeling that I didn't live up to her expectations of what a Christian woman should be.

I immediately took on guilt, assuming that I was indeed lacking in some way. After all, I knew how far from perfect I was—and am—and so I accepted her condemnation. I tried to win her approval, doing more for her, appreciating her more, giving her

113

more time and investing more in her life one way or another. But it was wasted effort.

Her condemnation was communicated through body language and general remarks. Even now it's difficult for me to pinpoint what she did that made me feel guilty. I can remember specific occasions when she subtly communicated her struggle to cope with me and all the problems that I brought into her life. She didn't say those words, but she sent that message, and I willingly heard it and accepted it.

Not until this woman left did I realize how miserable things had become as we spent time together. This dark cloud of condemnation just continued to get darker and heavier as time progressed, but I could not have told you what was happening. All I knew was that I felt guilty because no matter what I did, she was not pleased with me. And if she was not pleased with me, then obviously something was wrong with me and I needed to figure out what it was and fix it.

One evening I was invited to dinner at a friend's home and sat beside a man I had never met before (or since). I don't remember his name, but I could pick him out in a crowd, for I remember his face. And most of all I remember what he said to me. Though a lot of people were at this dinner, we were able to have a private conversation, and I discovered he was a Christian counselor who worked in some kind of ministry setting.

As our conversation continued, though I don't remember how the subject surfaced, he began to talk to me about people who have a victim mentality and find their identity in being a victim. Immediately his words struck a chord in my mind and I knew this was a message from God to me. I asked him questions about this type of person. He described someone with the same characteristics and attitudes of the person I was dealing with—and he didn't know a thing about her or me.

As I sat there, it was as though a veil were removed from my eyes and I could finally see what was happening. I am totally convinced that God's Spirit ordained this "chance" meeting and conversation to reveal a truth to me about accepting condemnation. I realized then that this person indeed found her whole identity in being a victim. If she wasn't being victimized, she manufactured it. And I realized at that moment that she could not accept that I was being good to her or trying to help her. She could only deal with life from a victim's perspective, and so she was a willing victim. That meant someone had to be victimizing her, and at the time, in her mind, that someone was me. Because I didn't understand the dynamics of the relationship, I allowed her to condemn me.

As I walked out of my friend's home that evening, I knew I was free. I can still remember the sense of relief and joy I felt because I now knew that I did not have to accept the guilt and condemnation this other person was trying to place on me. I had a choice, and I could choose to say no to her condemnation. From that moment on, I never accepted any more of her condemnation.

I never shared this with her, for I didn't see that it would do any good. But my attitude toward her and my demeanor in her presence changed, and she could not have missed the change. Shortly thereafter she went her way once more; that had been a pattern in her life. When I determined to stop accepting her condemnation, she chose to end the relationship.

No Condemnation

Romans 8:1-2 is a passage most Christians are familiar with and thankful for: "There is now no condemnation for those who are in Christ Jesus, because through Christ Jesus the law of the Spirit of life set me free from the law of sin and death."

No condemnation! What a wonderful truth. No other religion in the world offers this grace, for there is no other qualified savior except the Lord Jesus Christ. And because He took the condemnation that was due us, we can stand before a holy God without condemnation because God sees us in Christ, with His righteousness and without guilt. What a blessed salvation we have in Jesus!

Yet how many of us still accept condemnation that we put on ourselves or we allow others to put on us? Of course we're not perfect and there are things in our lives that need to be confronted and changed. But not condemned! No one has the right to condemn us except Jesus, and He doesn't.

Further on in Romans 8 we read:

> In face of all this, what is there left to say? If God is for us, who can be against us? He who did not hesitate to spare his own Son but gave him up for us all—can we not trust such a God to give us, with him, everything else that we can need? Who would dare to accuse us, whom God has chosen? The judge himself has declared us free from sin. Who is in a position to condemn? Only Christ, and Christ died for us, Christ rose for us, Christ reigns in power for us, Christ prays for us! (verses 31-34 PHILLIPS).

After my eye-opening conversation at dinner, I latched onto this passage for dear life. Time and again I would say to myself, *Mary, only Jesus can condemn you and He doesn't!* That has become a thought I've repeated to myself many times as I've had to continue applying the truth that God showed me that evening. Living free from condemnation is the freedom that Jesus came to give us. I don't want anything to ever rob me of that freedom again.

> **No one has the right to condemn us except Jesus, and He doesn't.**

Galatians 5:1 says, "It is for freedom that Christ has set us free. Stand firm, then, and do not let yourselves be burdened again by a yoke of slavery." You see, we can allow ourselves to be burdened again by a yoke of guilt and condemnation. You may be there now. Yet you also know that there is no condemnation for those in Christ Jesus, and you've reveled in that truth before. But for some reason you've allowed yourself to become burdened again by guilt.

The Circle of Freedom

Freedom from condemnation does not mean freedom from constructive criticism, but it does mean that we don't have to live under a cloud of condemnation from anyone, including ourselves. We must learn to apply this truth from Scripture. We have to retrain our thought patterns and learn to quickly recall this truth about condemnation. We have to stand firm, or, as the Phillips translation puts it, "Plant your feet firmly therefore within the freedom that Christ has won for us" (Galatians 5:1).

I love that imagery of planting your feet firmly within the freedom that Christ has won for you. Imagine that you are in a war and the enemy's fire is coming straight at you. Your commander says, "Come stand here in this circle, where you will be protected and the enemy's barrage cannot get to you. Just stay in this circle." Would you not run immediately to that circle and plant your feet firmly where you would be protected? Of course.

Well, can you not hear Jesus saying to you, "Here, come plant your feet firmly in the freedom that I have won for you. This battle has been fought and I won it. Come here and stand in this freedom that is now yours"? And our responsibility is to obey—to take our mental feet and plant them firmly in that circle of freedom. To bring our thoughts into the captivity of that Jesus-won freedom and refuse to let ourselves be burdened again by the slavery of guilt and condemnation.

In this challenge we face of managing guilt, we will have to learn to do this often. As the old saying goes, "You can't keep a bird from landing on your head, but you can keep him from building a nest there." You and I will not be able to eliminate all those thoughts and feelings of condemnation and guilt, but we can learn, by God's grace, to run into the circle of freedom that Jesus has won for us and plant our feet there.

Once again we recognize that this standing firm in the freedom that Christ has won for us is a mental activity. It all happens in our minds and therefore we must learn to take those condemning thoughts captive and make them obedient to Christ. Force them to be obedient to Christ. Refuse to let them take you back into slavery. Like any exercise, the more you do it, the easier it is to do. At first your thoughts will not willingly go into that circle of freedom. And once you get them there, they won't want to stay there very long. It is a mental battle, but if you're tired of being a slave to condemnation and guilt, you can learn to stand firm and refuse that yoke of slavery.

Talk Back to the Devil

A.W. Tozer, a great preacher of the last century, gave a sermon that became a book entitled *I Talk Back to the Devil.* That title alone gives us some good admonition, because we should learn to talk back to the devil. The Bible says, "Submit yourselves, then, to God. Resist the devil, and he will flee from you" (James 4:7). If you're learning to resist wrong thoughts and struggling with bringing those condemning thoughts into captivity, you will benefit greatly from talking back to the devil and repeating truths that can set you free. Truths such as...

- Only Jesus can condemn me, and He doesn't.
- I will not be burdened again with a yoke of slavery to guilt or condemnation.
- Jesus came to set me free from this guilt, and I choose to be free.
- You might as well give up, Satan, because I refuse to let you condemn me.

The best retort against the devil is Scripture. Memorizing Romans 8:1-2 is a very effective defense against the onslaught of the evil one:

> There is now no condemnation for those who are in
> Christ Jesus, because through Christ Jesus the law of the
> Spirit of life set me free from the law of sin and death.

Even if you don't memorize the exact words, you will know it well enough that you can paraphrase it back to the devil as a very powerful weapon against him.

Guilt and condemnation are weapons our enemy uses successfully because we allow him to. Why are we so susceptible? Because we know ourselves! We know the sins of our past, the repeated failures, the many shortcomings, and our enemy uses our knowledge for his onslaught against us. We actually provide him with the ammunition because we keep remembering what has been forgiven. We keep forgetting that we are acceptable to God because Jesus is acceptable to God. Our acceptance by God is not dependent on our performance.

Forgiving Ourselves

When we allow ourselves or others to condemn us, we are actually harboring unforgiveness in our heart toward ourselves. We don't think of that as wrong, but I ask you to recall the parable of the unmerciful servant, which appears in Matthew 18:23-35:

> The kingdom of heaven is like a king who wanted to settle accounts with his servants. As he began the settlement, a man who owed him ten thousand talents was brought to him. Since he was not able to pay, the master ordered that he and his wife and his children and all that he had be sold to repay the debt.
>
> The servant fell on his knees before him. "Be patient with me," he begged, "and I will pay back everything." The servant's master took pity on him, canceled the debt and let him go.
>
> But when that servant went out, he found one of his fellow servants who owed him a hundred denarii. He grabbed him and began to choke him. "Pay back what you owe me!" he demanded.
>
> His fellow servant fell to his knees and begged him, "Be patient with me, and I will pay you back."
>
> But he refused. Instead, he went off and had the man thrown into prison until he could pay the debt. When

the other servants saw what had happened, they were greatly distressed and went and told their master everything that had happened.

Then the master called the servant in. "You wicked servant," he said, "I canceled all that debt of yours because you begged me to. Shouldn't you have had mercy on your fellow servant just as I had on you?" In anger his master turned him over to the jailers to be tortured, until he should pay back all he owed.

This is how my heavenly Father will treat each of you unless you forgive your brother from your heart.

You may be thinking, how does that parable relate to self-condemnation? Well, can it be any less important for you and me to forgive ourselves than it is for us to forgive others? Is it any less sinful to hold a grudge against yourself, so to speak, than to hold grudges and unforgiveness in your heart toward others?

Notice that the unforgiving servant—the one who had been forgiven so much—was turned over to be tortured. I am convinced that much of the torture and torment that many of us carry is because we have allowed ourselves to hold grudges and harbor unforgiveness toward ourselves. Did Jesus pay the price for our sins past and present? He did. Was the price He paid satisfactory to His Father? It was. Can any amount of self-torment or abuse that we inflict upon ourselves make us more acceptable to God? Never. Why then do we allow the enemy of our soul to continue to defeat us with condemnation?

Colossians 3:13 tells us to "bear with each other and forgive whatever grievances you may have against one another. Forgive as the Lord forgave you." I am told that the phrase "one another" in the original Greek text is *heautou,* which includes the reader as the object of the forgiveness and can be translated "yourselves." Let's paraphrase the verse so it accentuates that truth: "Bear with yourself and forgive yourself whatever grievance you may have against yourself. Forgive as the Lord forgave you."

We know that lack of forgiveness toward others hinders our relationship with God, creates bitterness, and opens the door for the enemy of our soul to torment us. And the same is true when we refuse to forgive ourselves. Hebrews 12:15 warns us to "see to it…that no bitter root grows up to cause trouble and defile many." Harboring unforgiveness toward ourselves is a breeding ground for bitterness, which defiles us. And spiritual defilement, in turn, opens us up to the attacks of the enemy and his demons. We become easy targets for spiritual defeat.

Who Condemns You?

From whom have you been accepting condemnation? It could be someone from your childhood years, and you've been carrying that condemnation around in your backpack ever since. Someone said something that condemned you, perhaps only once or maybe over a long period of time, and you accepted it. As a child, you wouldn't have known any better to determine whether you were innocent or guilty. So the cloud of condemnation has hung over your head since. Perhaps your recollection of that condemnation is only occasional, but it does surface, and you can hear those words of condemnation as though they were said yesterday.

You may have accepted condemnation from an authority figure in your life—a boss, a pastor, a parent, an uncle or aunt, an older sibling. Authority figures can have a great influence on us because of their status, and thus their words of condemnation can affect us deeply. A woman recently wrote me about her boss, who lays small condemnations on her regularly—negative comments and sarcastic gibes obviously meant to hurt her. She wrote, "My frustration and anger are building and my confidence is shaken." She's ready to resign a job she once loved all because of condemning words spoken by her boss—and, by the way, she works for a Christian organization.

Are you guilty of laying condemnation on yourself? I don't mean just accepting it; I mean creating it *and* accepting it. It happens when your thoughts are out of control and you allow yourself to dwell on your past and on those wrong messages. It happens when you fall into the comparison trap, when you try to please everyone, and when you live with unrealistic expectations of yourself. The longer you have indulged in these wrong thought patterns, the more your enemy has succeeded in building a stronghold in your life that keeps you mired in guilt.

The good news is that you can choose to walk into that circle of freedom right now, today. It is for freedom that Christ came to set you free. I pray that you will recognize any area of condemnation, from yourself or others, and determine by God's grace to throw it overboard right now. And every time it raises its ugly head again, that you will replace those wrong thoughts with truths from God's Word.

Growing Free from Guilt

1. Who have you allowed to condemn you in the past?
   - ❏ A parent
   - ❏ A sibling
   - ❏ A child
   - ❏ A boss
   - ❏ A friend
   - ❏ Your mate
   - ❏ Yourself
   - ❏ Other: _____

   (Please be as specific as you can in identifying the sources of condemnation. That will make it much easier for you to free yourself from that condemnation.)

2. If you need to apologize or ask for forgiveness, have you done that yet?
   - ❏ Yes
   - ❏ No

   If not, are you willing to take those steps at this time?
   - ❏ Yes
   - ❏ No

   If no, why not?

3. If you recognize that you have been under self-condemnation, please pray along these lines every day for a month:

   Dear Lord, for too long I have wallowed in self-condemnation and refused to walk into the freedom that You died to give me. Please forgive me for not forgiving myself. Teach me how to bear with myself and forgive the grievances I have against myself. You have forgiven me, and I have no right to withhold forgiveness from myself. I want to live in Your circle of freedom. Please help me to do that today. Amen.

4. Memorize Romans 8:1-2 and quote these verses every morning: "There is now no condemnation for those who are

in Christ Jesus, because through Christ Jesus the law of the Spirit of life set me free from the law of sin and death."

5. Determine that you will talk back to the devil when he tries to lay condemnation on you. Determine what you will say to him, using one of these suggestions or a truth of your own:

- Only Jesus can condemn me, and He doesn't.
- I will not be burdened again with a yoke of slavery to guilt or condemnation.
- Jesus came to set me free from this guilt, and I choose to be free.
- You may as well give up, Satan, because I refuse to let you condemn me.

10

The Guilt
Is Gone

As you read through the Old Testament—and I highly recommend that you do!—you'll discover that guilt is a very common topic. In fact, one resource tells me there are 167 references to guilt in the Old Testament compared to only 16 in the New Testament.[4] Leviticus, the third book in the Old Testament, has by far the most references to guilt—a total of 38. That's because Leviticus is primarily a book of laws, containing material revealed at Sinai after the children of Israel left Egypt and before they began their 40-year wilderness wanderings.

Quite frankly, if you're having trouble getting to sleep at night, you might try reading Leviticus as you go to bed. It is similar to reading all the legalese that we typically skip when signing official documents! Yet there it is in God's inspired Word, and Romans 15:4 says that "everything that was written in the past was written to teach us, so that through endurance and the encouragement of the Scriptures we might have hope."

I admit that in the past, I'd often wondered what real benefit there was in reading Leviticus, so I read it mostly so I could say I'd read it! Finally it dawned on me that it was important for me to understand what is was like to live in a totally legalistic world—constantly trying to perform up to God's specific standards and constantly failing. No wonder guilt is frequently addressed under the Old Covenant, when God's people were trying to live by the law. It's only when I understand the burden (and impossibility) of trying to live up to God's holy requirements that I can appreciate the free gift of the righteousness of Jesus Christ, which is mine because Jesus paid the price for my sins. And because I have His righteousness, I am righteous in the sight of our holy God—and set free from legalism!

You may be wondering why God would give the Israelites a law to live by if He knew full well they couldn't live up to it. The books of Romans and Galatians address this issue in depth, and it is a study worth pursuing. Suffice it to say that the law was given to show us that we cannot justify ourselves by living up to the law.

> **Truth sets us free, but we have to know it and hold to it before it can do that.**

Paul wrote, "The law was put in charge to lead us to Christ that we might be justified by faith. Now that faith has come, we are no longer under the supervision of the law" (Galatians 3:24-25).

Before Christ came, God's people needed some way to deal with the guilt of their sin. So, guilt offerings were established as part of the law. There are 26 references in Leviticus to guilt offerings and how they were to be given. Reading Leviticus reminds us that guilt has plagued mankind since the Garden of Eden. It was such a big issue that much of the law given by God through Moses dealt with guilt and how to get rid of it.

So why am I referring to guilt offerings of the Old Covenant when we've just read from Galatians 3 that we are no longer under the supervision of the law? Because even Leviticus was written to teach us and to give us hope, and there is a wonderful teaching given in Leviticus concerning the Day of Atonement which has taught me much about letting go of guilt and given me great hope. I want to share that teaching with you because I believe it can have the same benefit for you.

What I'm about to share pertains to what we call Bible doctrine, and too often we think doctrine is the realm of Bible teachers, preachers, seminary students, and the like. That is unfortunate because when we have a more in-depth knowledge of doctrine, which is simply biblical truth, we have a more sure foundation for our faith that brings us freedom and joy. Jesus said, "If you hold to my teaching, you are really my disciples. Then you will know the truth, and the truth will set you free" (John 8:31-32). Truth sets us free, but we have to know it and hold to it before it can do that. This means we have to dig into these Bible doctrines that can offer us freedom.

Pictures from the Past

As I already mentioned, the teaching I want to share has to do with the Day of Atonement. I'm now going to present the story of the Day of Atonement as a drama in five acts to help make it as easy to understand as possible—even if you do not have much Bible knowledge. As you read this story, please try to put yourself in the picture. Imagine that you are one of the people of Israel. You're trying to live up to the law and frequently failing, and thus you are in desperate need of some way to deal with the aftermath of guilt. Once a year, on the Day of Atonement, the high priest engaged in a ritual that was intended to help rid the people of their guilt.

The Day of Atonement: A Drama in Five Acts
Act 1: The High Priest Goes to the Tabernacle

Setting

In the Old Testament, the function of the priests was similar to that of lawyers today. They represented the people to God and spoke to God on their behalf. Before the temple was built, the priests operated in a mobile worship center called the tabernacle, which was separated into different areas by curtains and contained various pieces of symbolic furniture and implements.

At the center of the tabernacle was the Most Holy Place, which was screened off from view by a heavy curtain. Only the high priest was allowed to enter into the Most Holy Place. In it was the Ark of the Covenant—a wooden chest carried on poles.

Rising from the lid of the chest were two golden statues of cherubim. We think of cherubim as cute little angelic things used for decoration. But understand that these cherubim were big and awesome and intimidating because they represented the judgment of God. In the Bible our first introduction to cherubim occurs at the entrance to the Garden of Eden. They were stationed there to prevent Adam and Eve from re-entering into the presence of God after they sinned and were put out of the Garden. The golden cherubim on top of the Ark of the Covenant served as a visual reminder that no one could come near God without coming close to judgment.

The mercy seat was a flat area between the cherubim, and that is where God told Moses He would meet with him: "There, above the cover between the two cherubim that are over the ark of the Testimony, I will meet with you and give you all my commands for the Israelites" (Exodus 25:22).

Only once a year, on the Day of Atonement, could the high priest enter into this Most Holy Place. God would come down, just as He had done on Mount Sinai, but He did not make Himself visible; He appeared in a cloud. The cherubim and the mercy seat symbolized that God met with the high priest—and through the high priest, the people of God—at a place that spoke of mercy and judgment.

Costumes

The high priest was one of the most important people in the whole nation. His clothes sent that message. These clothes displayed the dignity of his office. Rich in symbolism, his breastplate contained 12 precious stones representing the 12 tribes of Israel. He wore a sleeveless tunic of fine linen that was decorated with gold, blue, purple, and scarlet trim. Seeing the high priest in his full attire would be like seeing royalty on a state occasion.

But on the Day of Atonement, the high priest did not wear his usual uniform. He set aside his magnificent clothes and appeared in the streets wearing a simple white cloth instead. He dressed as a lowly servant would.

So, as our play opens, the high priest, the man who holds the most prominent and dignified office in the land, appears dressed as a common slave. He begins making his way to the tabernacle, and the people crowd around to watch. They know from his change in dress that this is a most important day.

Act 2: *The High Priest Prepares*

Aaron, Moses' brother, was the first high priest. But Aaron himself was a sinner, as was every high priest who followed him. Remember how Aaron had sinned and broken the law when he made the golden calf for the Israelites to worship (see Exodus 32). He was not a perfect man.

So, before he or any other high priest could enter the presence of God to deal with the sins of the people, he had to deal with his own sins first. According to Leviticus 16, Aaron had to sacrifice a bull for his own sin offering. So in this second act, we see the high priest take some of the blood from the sacrificed bull, go past the curtain into the Most Holy Place, and sprinkle the blood on the mercy seat as a sacrifice for his own sins.

Act 3: *Atonement Is Made*

Next the high priest comes back out of the tabernacle, and two goats are brought to him. One of these goats is for a sacrifice for the sin of the people, and the other is what's known as a scapegoat. The high priest kills the sacrificial goat and, once again takes some of the blood into the Most Holy Place and sprinkles it on the mercy seat. This is done for the sins of all the other people.

It's important to get the picture here: The mercy seat is the flat surface between the figures of the cherubim. God's agents of judgment are looking down at the mercy seat. When the high priest sprinkles the blood on the mercy seat, it is as if judgment and mercy are meeting together. Judgment, which demands death as the penalty for sin, is satisfied; mercy, which demands forgiveness for the sinner, is sustained. Mercy is released in the place of judgment as the blood is sprinkled.

Why did blood have to be sprinkled on the mercy seat? It demonstrated that a death had taken place. God made it clear to Adam that the consequence of sin is death. On the Day of Atonement God allowed the death sentence for people to be transferred onto an animal. It was a visual statement that sins and guilt could not be removed until blood was shed. God's judgment demanded a blood sacrifice from the sinner—death. God's mercy accepted a substitute sacrifice—allowing the sinner to live.

Now, suppose the high priest decided to bring something else into the Most Holy Place instead of blood. After all, this was a pretty gruesome ordeal, killing animals and sprinkling blood. Suppose he brought in a vial of tears representing the repentance of the people. "Lord, I'm sprinkling these tears on the mercy seat this time—not the messy blood—because your people have shed these tears in repentance of their sins. Please let their tears of repentance satisfy your judgment."

Or suppose the high priest had brought rags soaked in sweat. "Lord, instead of blood, I'm wiping the mercy seat with these rags filled with sweat because your people have worked really hard and they have done lots of good things, and they've tried to be good people. Let their good deeds satisfy your demands for justice."

Neither of those alternatives would have worked. Nothing could satisfy God's justice except a perfect sacrifice for sin. Blood had to be shed. Nothing else the high priest could bring into the Most Holy Place would pay the debt that justice demanded.

This entire ritual was a picture of what Messiah would do for His people when He came to redeem them from their sins.

God's justice is not satisfied by our tears of repentance or by the strength of our effort. Atonement for our sins is only possible through the blood of Jesus Christ, shed for us, meeting God's demand for justice and opening up the floodgates of God's mercy and grace for all who believe.

Act 4: Sin Is Confessed

After sprinkling the blood of the sacrificial goat on the mercy seat for the sins of the people, the high priest comes out of the Most Holy Place. Then the second goat is brought to him. As Leviticus 16: 21 says, "He is to lay both hands on the head of the live goat and confess over it all the wickedness and rebellion of the Israelites—all their sins—and put them on the goat's head."

At this point the high priest confesses all the sins of Israel while laying his hands on the head of the live goat. Are you picturing this scene? The high priest is holding this squirming, noisy, bucking goat with both hands on his head, and confessing out loud all the sins of the people. What a scene that must have been! No matter how solemn the occasion was to the people, the goat would not have been solemn. It was not a simple thing for the high priest to hold that goat while confessing all the people's sins.

What's more, imagine all the sins he would have to confess: idolatry, envy, adultery, anger, selfishness, unkindness, stealing, lying, pride, greed, and so on. This would have been a long prayer. The priest had to pray in such a way that the people recognized the specific sins that needed to be confessed. Imagine that you are watching all this and listening to the litany of sins that the high priest is confessing. When he mentions your sins, would you not flinch a bit? Can't you imagine everyone listening in silence, with bowed heads, embarrassed to know that their sins are part of this ritual?

To get a deeper understanding of what this scene must have engendered in the hearts of the people who watched this drama unfold, just imagine your pastor standing in front of your church next Sunday and saying, "I am now going to pray for all the sins of our congregation this past week." And then he begins to pray, "Dear God, we confess that we are proud people. This week we have spoken harsh words, we have had angry hearts, we have been upset when we didn't get our way, we have lied and not always told the truth, we have cheated our employers, we have been unkind to our family members, we have had lousy negative attitudes, we have lost our temper, we have been unfaithful to our mates, we have committed fornication, we have loved other things and other people more than You..." and on and on the prayer goes. Don't you think the people would get rather quiet and feel a little uneasy as these specific sins are confessed? I might be thinking, *Who told him what I did this week? Who's the snitch?* That would be a humbling experience, don't you think?

This was necessary, however, no matter how uncomfortable it was. Sin cannot be atoned for and forgiven until it is confessed and forsaken. It was as true then as it is today. So, by God's design, when the high priest confessed the sins of the people with his hands on the head of the goat, an act of transfer took place. God "moved" the guilt of those sins onto the goat. God regarded those sins as being placed on the head of the goat and being carried by it—as though the goat had committed all those sins.

You say, "That's not fair; that goat is innocent of all those sins." That's right! The sins of the people were transferred to an innocent goat. He hadn't committed any of those sins, but they were placed on him.

That's a picture of what our Lord did when He died on the cross for our sins. All our sins were transferred to Jesus that day at Calvary. That's why God the Father turned His back on God the Son as He hung on that cross—because God the Father could not look on sin, and Jesus had all the sins of the world on Him that day.

- 2 Corinthians 5:21: "God made him [Jesus] who had no sin to be sin for us, so that in him we might become the righteousness of God."

- 1 Peter 2:24: "He himself bore our sins in his body on the tree, so that we might die to sins and live for righteousness; by his wounds you have been healed."

This was the terrible ordeal that Jesus dreaded when He prayed in the Garden of Gethsemane: "Father, if you are willing, take this cup from me; yet not my will, but yours be done" (Luke 22:42). The physical pain and disgrace of death on the cross, as awful as it was, was not what Jesus wanted to avoid. Others had died that death and He could do that, too. But never before had He been separated from His Father, and the knowledge that God the Father would have to forsake Him as He became sin for us was what He dreaded.

Picturing the sins of the people of Israel being transferred by the high priest to that innocent goat gives me a "handle" for better understanding what Jesus did for me. At one and the same time, I am so grateful that He was willing to bear my sins, which brings me great joy and comfort, and I am also so ashamed and saddened that my sins were part of the cross He bore at Calvary.

Act 5: Guilt Is Removed

In this final act of our drama, after the high priest's confession, the high priest sends the guilty goat into the desert. Leviticus 16:21-22 says, "He shall send the goat away into the desert in the care of a man appointed for the task. The goat will carry on itself all their sins to a solitary place; and the man shall release it in the desert." A man was designated to lead that goat way out into the desert and then let it go so the goat is gone forever. It will be remembered no more.

Imagine yourself in that crowd. After hearing your sins confessed, you watch the "guilty" goat being led away until you could not see it anymore. Along with the rest of the crowd, you stand on your tiptoes and watch for a long time as the goat becomes smaller and smaller on the horizon. Then the goat is gone, taking with it all those sins that were symbolically heaped on its head and all the guilt that went with those sins.

Can you not imagine the relief that must have surged through the crowd as they once again realized that God had made provision for their sin and their guilt? All year long they've waited for the Day of Atonement—the day when they could put behind them the sins and guilt of the preceding year and not have to worry about them again. The price was paid, the blood was shed, the guilt was gone!

Truths for Today

The events of the Day of Atonement were essentially a series of visual aids in which God taught some basic truths we need to grasp:

1. We need a priest who will lay aside his dignity and honor and come as a servant to make atonement for us.
2. That priest needs to be prepared, because a man encumbered by his own sins cannot atone for the sins of others.
3. Atonement can be made only by the shedding of blood. This satisfies the justice of God, allowing mercy to be released to the people.
4. Sin must be confessed, and when it is, its guilt will be transferred.
5. When atonement has been made and sin has been confessed, then your guilt will be removed. It will be taken out of your sight.

The Day of Atonement is a preview of what Christ did for us.

Act 1: Christ Appears

Philippians 2:6-7 says, "[Jesus], being in very nature God, did not consider equality with God something to be grasped, but made himself nothing, taking the very nature of a servant, being made in human likeness." Jesus set aside His magnificent clothing, His glory, and took the form of a servant. He wore strips of cloth as a baby in a manger. This is the High Priest who descended from His exalted position and humbled Himself, giving Himself completely to others.

Act 2: Christ Is Prepared

Jesus lived a perfect life. No one could accuse Him of sin. He did not need to offer a sacrifice for His own sin, for He committed no sin. Hebrews 7:26-27 says of Jesus,

> Such a high priest meets our need—one who is holy, blameless, pure, set apart from sinners, exalted above the heavens. Unlike the other high priests, he does not need to offer sacrifices day after day, first for his own sins, and then for the sins of the people. He sacrificed for their sins once for all when he offered himself.

Jesus was what no other high priest ever was or could be—sinless. He was and is a qualified Savior.

Act 3: Christ Makes Atonement

Christ's blood was shed on Calvary; the judgment of God fell on Him. Darkness covered the face of the earth. The inner curtain of the temple was ripped from top to bottom, exposing the Most Holy Place. Now because of Jesus, the High Priest who atoned for our sins, a new and living way was opened for us into the presence of God. No longer is the Most Holy Place reserved for one man once a year. Now we have access to God's throne, right into the Holy of Holies, because Jesus paid the price to open the door to God for us. Hebrews 4:16 says, "Let us then approach the throne of grace with confidence, so that we may receive mercy and find grace to help us in our time of need."

Act 4: We Confess Our Sins

Remember there were two goats on the Day of Atonement: one was killed, and the other was led into the desert. Both help us to understand what Christ does for His people. He is the one who was sacrificed for our sins, and He is also the one who is able to take away our guilt.

Just as the high priest had to confess the sins of the people, now we must confess our sins. This is absolutely essential. We must confess our sins and recognize that in so doing, they are being transferred to Christ—that they are being included in the sin for which He died.

Act 5: Our Sins Are Removed

When John the Baptist saw Jesus, he said, "Look, the Lamb of God, who takes away the sin of the world!" (John 1:29). Everyone who heard that would have understood exactly what John meant because they had witnessed the Day of Atonement many times and seen that goat led away with all their sins heaped on its head. Unless you understand what the Day of Atonement signifies, you miss the incredible truth of this proclamation. Can you imagine what the people who heard John the Baptist must have thought when he announced that Jesus was like that scapegoat—He was God's Scapegoat sent to take away our sin and guilt? No doubt some were puzzled by John's statement, and others were angered and bothered, thinking it blasphemous. But surely some must have rejoiced to think that God had finally sent Messiah, the one who would be the perfect sacrifice so that once and for all their sins could be atoned and their guilt could be removed.

Can you see your sins laid on Jesus as you lay hold of Him in faith and confess your sins? Can you picture your specific sins being taken away into the distance and out of sight? Can you believe that through the finished work of Christ your sins are not only forgiven but your guilt is also removed?

We no longer need a Day of Atonement, or sacrificial bulls or goats, or an earthly high priest to intercede for us. Jesus is our once-and-for-all sacrifice, and He is also our High Priest. No longer do we need a ritual to remind us that a Messiah is coming to redeem us because Messiah has already come and redeemed us. Hebrews 10:11-14 says,

Day after day every priest stands and performs his religious duties; again and again he offers the same sacrifices, which can never take away sins. But when this priest [Jesus Christ] had offered for all time one sacrifice for sins, he sat down at the right hand of God. Since that time he waits for his enemies to be made his footstool, because by one sacrifice he has made perfect forever those who are being made holy.

The only thing left for us to do is to decide whether we believe this to be true, and if so, to make certain our sins have been confessed and transferred to Jesus. Upon becoming a child of God through faith in Jesus Christ, our challenge is to live in the freedom purchased for us by Jesus when He died and rose again. We must recognize that our sin and guilt have been taken away, never to be remembered against us again.

- *Psalm 103:10-12:* "He [the Lord] does not treat us as our sins deserve or repay us according to our iniquities. For as high as the heavens are above the earth, so great is his love for those who fear him; as far as the east is from the west, so far has he removed our transgressions from us."
- *Isaiah 43:25:* "I, even I, am he who blots out your transgressions, for my own sake, and remembers your sins no more."

Our Guilt Is Gone!

How it must grieve the heart of our loving Father when He sees His children continuing to live under a load of guilt for sins that have been confessed, forgiven, and blotted out! Instead of rejoicing in the unspeakable gift that is ours through Christ, we keep reliving the past, remembering what God has chosen to forget. And we lose sight of the biblical truth that our guilt is gone because our sins are forgiven.

Sometimes when we ask a person for forgiveness, it is given to us, but later on the person reminds us of our transgression (or we remind ourselves) and the guilt of that mistake continues to haunt us. What kind of forgiveness is that? It's not the way God forgives us, that's for sure. He remembers our sins no more. Though we may live with some consequences of our sin, God never brings it up again to beat us over the head with it. Never! Once it is confessed, it is forgiven.

If you are still living with guilt from past sins that have been confessed, forsaken, and forgiven, it is because you choose to. You choose to keep heaping guilt on yourself; that guilt is not from God.

Shortly after my decision to renew my relationship with Jesus and give Him control of my life, I was spending time in prayer when, suddenly, scenes of past sins were flashing through my mind as if I were watching a slide show. And once again I felt the shame and guilt of that past. I began to confess those sins to God again: "Lord, I'm so sorry for what I did! How could I ever have done those things!" As those thoughts were going through my mind, I clearly sensed God's still, quiet voice in my mind saying, "I don't know what you're talking about." God chooses to remember our sins no more, and even when we keep regurgitating them, He reminds us that the guilt is gone and that it is not profitable or proper for us to wallow in the past. Our guilt is gone, and we should live in that freedom.

Growing Free from Guilt

1. Imagine yourself as part of the crowd in ancient Israel, watching this drama of the Day of Atonement. You know that the high priest must first offer a sacrifice for his own sins before he can offer a sacrifice for the sins of the people. What impression would this have made on you and the others who were watching?

   ❏ I would have wondered how someone who is a sinner himself could be an advocate to God for my sins.

   ❏ I would have felt even greater guilt, for if the high priest (who surely is better than me) had to offer a sacrifice for his sins, how much worse of a sinner am I when compared to him?

   ❏ I would have wondered what made the high priest so qualified to go into the Most Holy Place, because he was a sinner like me.

   ❏ Other: _____

2. Can you recall the time when you consciously confessed your sins to God and knew that they were transferred to Jesus, believed that Jesus did indeed pay the price for your atonement, and knew from that moment forward that you were now made righteous in Christ Jesus?

   ❏ Yes
   ❏ No

3. If yes, when did that happen? _____

   _____

4. If no, please read the appendix, which will help you understand exactly what to do in order to be forgiven and made righteous in Christ Jesus.

11

Managing Your
Guilt

Guilt is a feeling, whether accurate or inaccurate. And our guilt feelings are formed by our thoughts and our thought patterns. If we're ever going to be able to manage our feelings of guilt and have victory over them consistently, we will have to learn how to bring our thought life under the control of God's Spirit.

As I said in chapter 1, I would be skeptical of anyone who claimed to live a guilt-free life. In my opinion they would be living in deception or oblivion! James 3:2 reminds us that "we all stumble in many ways. If anyone is never at fault in what he says, he is a perfect man, able to keep his whole body in check." Because all of us are susceptible to stumbling, and as far as I know none of us is perfect, we are all susceptible to feeling guilty.

Our challenge is to learn how to manage our feelings of guilt and deal with them in biblical ways that lead us to freedom. Galatians 5:1 says, "It is for freedom that Christ has set us free. Stand firm, then, and do not let yourselves be burdened again by a yoke of slavery." When we struggle with guilt, we place ourselves in a yoke of slavery that burdens us and strangles us and keeps us in bondage.

Dealing with Guilt: The Options

What options do we have when we are plagued with feelings of guilt? I'll use an example that can be classified as both true and false guilt:

A young Christian woman becomes pregnant out of wedlock, and with the counsel of friends and family, decides to give her child up for adoption. She is plagued with true guilt because of her choice to have a sexual relationship outside of marriage, and she is plagued with false guilt for, as she sees it, abandoning her baby.

Option #1: She can allow her thoughts to continually condemn her.

Thoughts of her sexual indiscretion flood her mind at the most unexpected times. She blames herself over and over for allowing that man or boy to talk her into something she promised would never happen to her. She replays the tape in her mind of that night or that affair, and feels dirty and unlovable as a result. The images of the sexual encounter(s) bombard her, even when she is trying to pray. She thinks of the baby she gave up, and her arms long to hold him or her. She wonders if that was the right decision. She feels like a total failure; after all, what kind of woman would give up her baby?

Option #2: She can try to shift the blame.

In trying to cope with the overwhelming feelings of guilt, she tries to blame her circumstances and rationalizes all of what happened. After all, she was not raised in a strong Christian home, she didn't have a good support group, and she was certainly a lot more circumspect than most of her friends, who had multiple sexual partners. With casual sex so prevalent and acceptable in contemporary society, how could she be blamed for what she did? And besides, she may rationalize, she's not as strong or as smart as other women.

Option #3: She can try to drown the guilt.

Overwhelming feelings of guilt are one major cause of addictions. And there are many addictive behaviors available to her, so she tries one of them. It could be alcohol or drugs or eating or shopping, to name the most common ones.

Option #4: She can punish herself.

Depending on the extent of her guilt feelings, she may go so far as to decide that she can never think of being married or having other children because she doesn't deserve any happiness or fulfillment after what she has done. Or she may conclude that the only kind of man of whom she is worthy is a worthless kind of man, so she becomes involved with losers because she thinks she doesn't deserve any better. Self-punishment can also take the form of abuse to her body, lack of care for her personal health or her looks, or refusing to pursue educational goals or career dreams because she feels she is not worthy.

Option #5: She can face the music and move on.

Face the music and move on—six little words that represent some significant mental work and discipline. But considering the consequences of the other options, this is the only one that makes sense.

Dealing with Guilt: A Plan

Let's assume this young woman chooses option #5—she's willing to do the hard work required in order to put this behind her and move on to the good things God has for her life. This means she will need a plan for guilt management because this is not going to happen overnight. She will have to be intentional about this or her good intentions will take her nowhere.

Using our hypothetical guilt-ridden woman as an example—we'll call her "Jennifer"—who is dealing with both true and false guilt, let's lay out a specific plan of action for her. These principles for managing guilt apply to every kind of guilt that might plague us—whether true or false guilt, major or minor guilt, long-term or short-term, intermittent or constant, these principles will help you take positive biblical steps toward dealing with your guilt. We've already seen some of these suggestions earlier in this book, but I want to put them together here so we can see, in one place, clear guidance on getting rid of guilt and living in the freedom that Christ came to give us.

Please understand that I'm not suggesting that it's as easy as ABC—just follow these how-to steps and, voilà, you'll be guilt-free! The Christian life and our faith journey is not a formula that can produce guaranteed results; I know that full well. That would take us right back into a legalistic lifestyle. We are each unique creations of our heavenly Father, and He works in our lives in His own endless variety of ways that are best suited to each of us.

But I also know that until we become intentional about applying biblical truths and principles to our lives, we will never reap the benefits of these truths. And I see so many people who just don't know how to get started, or who lack the experience of learning to apply God's Word in practical ways. So, for that reason, I want to give a how-to type of plan for guilt management. This is not a magic wand that leads to instant success. But because this plan is based on biblical principles, I am confident it will be helpful.

Accept Responsibility

Jennifer must accept the responsibility that is hers, without excuses, and openly and specifically confess the sin that caused the true guilt she is dealing with. She needs to pray along these lines:

> Father God, I acknowledge my sin that has caused this heavy load of guilt. I sinned against You and I sinned against the Holy Spirit within me when I chose to have sexual relations outside of marriage. I knew it was wrong when I did it, and I knew I should not have done it. This was my sin, and even if others contributed or participated in it, I could have chosen not to sin; I could have taken the way of escape that you always provide with every temptation, as promised in 1 Corinthians 10:13. Please forgive me for this transgression of your principles. I know you give me principles for my life for my own good, and when I choose to disobey, there are consequences.

However, I gladly claim your promise that when I confess my sin, You are faithful and just to forgive me of all my sins and purify me from all unrighteousness (1 John 1:9). I thank You that I am now forgiven, and that this sin is remembered against me no more (Isaiah 43:25). Thank you, Jesus, for having paid the price demanded by God's holiness so that my guilt can be taken away. Thank you that my sin has been taken away as far as the east is from the west (Psalm 103:12). I pray in Jesus' name, amen.

> **It is important to base our prayers on God's Word, for then we can be certain that we have prayed correctly.**

Jennifer may or may not have some emotional feeling of relief after this prayer of confession, but if she prayed in faith, then her guilt is gone. It is important to base our prayers on God's Word, for then we can be certain that we have prayed correctly. In her prayer, Jennifer referenced four promises in Scripture on which she based her prayer and her hope. I cannot overemphasize how important it is to learn to base your prayers on God's Word. When you pray in this way, your faith is rooted firmly in what God has said, and this will bring you comfort and hope.

Change Your Thought Patterns

The challenge Jennifer now faces is to live in the truth of what has happened. Her sin has been forgiven, so there's no reason for her to continue feeling guilty. But because her thoughts have been so long in the rut of blaming herself and feeling guilty, it may take time for her to adjust. She must confront these negative thought patterns and, by God's grace, change them. You can be certain that the enemy of her soul is not going to give up easily. He has used guilt to debilitate her and depress her and discourage her and has made deep inroads into her thought life. He knows the buttons to push, and he'll do whatever he can to get her back into the rut of guilt.

Merely *telling* Jennifer to change her thought patterns is not enough. She needs to be prepared with a biblical method for bringing her wrong thoughts under control. And for sure, God's Word gives us the tools we need for this. Here is the core ingredient that Jennifer must apply to her thought life:

> We demolish arguments and every pretension that sets itself up against the knowledge of God, and we take captive every thought to make it obedient to Christ (2 Corinthians 10:5).

Jennifer will now be battling the "arguments and every pretension" of the enemy of her soul who will set these arguments up against what she knows to be true from God's Word. It's the same thing the enemy did to Eve in the Garden of Eden: He questioned God's Word and caused Eve to doubt what God had said. He asked Eve, "Did God really say…?" (Genesis 3:1). All it took was that one seed of doubt to cause Eve to come under his spell and disobey God. So Jennifer must be prepared for the attacks the enemy will bring through her thought life. As soon as she realizes her thoughts are taking her away from the freedom she has in Christ, then she must take those thoughts captive and force them to be obedient to Christ.

Here's the most important principle to remember when you are trying to change long-held thought patterns: You have to replace wrong thoughts with right thoughts. It's not enough to tell yourself to stop thinking those wrong thoughts. You have to fill your mind with right thinking so that there is no room for wrong thinking. Remember, as Jesus told us, the truth sets us free, and thinking upon God's truth is how Jennifer can be freed from her wrong thoughts.

In chapter 8 I provided a list of scriptures you can memorize in response to the wrong messages that might arise in your mind. Bible truths and promises are the best replacement thoughts you'll ever find. If Jennifer memorizes a few verses or becomes so familiar with them that she can easily paraphrase them, then she can be ready with a response when the enemy tries to destroy her faith with the thought, *You don't really believe God just forgave you for that sin and doesn't remember anymore, do you?* She can quote Isaiah 43:25 and remind herself of the truth that God promises to remember her sins against her no more. She may need to repeat this several times in order to drown out the wrong thought, but the Word of God is powerful and it can defeat wrong thoughts more completely and quickly than anything else. Hebrews 4:12 tells us, "The word of God is living and active. Sharper than any double-edged sword, it penetrates even to dividing soul and spirit, joints and marrow; it judges the thoughts and attitudes of the heart."

We have the weapon we need to win the war against wrong thought patterns. We just need to know how to use it.

Praise God for Victory over Your Guilt

Jennifer now needs to talk and live as though this victory is complete, for indeed it is complete in Christ. She must defeat the negative attitudes and feelings by megadoses of praise. There are incredible promises God gives for those who are people of praise, and praise takes many forms.

Praise Through Thanksgiving

Praise can take the form of thankfulness. For example, "I will give thanks to the LORD because of his righteousness and will sing praise to the name of the LORD Most High" (Psalm 7:17). Jennifer needs to start thanking God for His goodness to her. She needs to be specific in her praise of thanksgiving: "I thank You for my salvation, my good health, my trusted friends," and so on.

Praise Through Song

Music is another wonderful avenue of praise. Psalm 30:4 says, "Sing to the LORD, you saints of his; praise his holy name." Jennifer needs to sing songs of praise as much as she can during the day. She needs to keep her radio tuned to Christian stations that play God-focused music, play praise CDs at every opportunity and sing along with them, and simply sing praise to God.

Praise Through Adoration

One way to praise God is to recite the wonders that He has done. Psalm 9:1 says, "I will praise you, O LORD, with all my heart; I will tell of all your wonders." Jennifer needs to praise God daily for the beauty of His creation and all the wonders of the universe that are around her. She also needs to praise God for the wonders in her own life, the wonderful things He has done for her.

Praise at All Times

Praise is not reserved solely for special times; it is to be practiced all the time. Psalm 34:1 says, "I will extol the LORD at all times; his praise will always be on my lips." Jennifer needs to become intentional about praising God for every little thing throughout her day—for the sunshine, for the good parking place, for accomplishing a task, for a friend, for her paycheck, for everything all day long. Becoming a woman of praise will make a huge difference in her thought life and play a major role in helping to change her wrong thought patterns.

Praise in Corporate Worship

Corporate praise is important. Psalm 68:25 says, "Praise God in the great congregation; praise the Lord in the assembly of Israel." Jennifer needs to be involved in a body of believers in a good church where she can praise God with others.

The phrase "praise the LORD" appears 188 times in the Bible, and over half are in the psalms, most of them written by King David. No wonder he was a man after God's own heart—he was a man of praise. In spite of the troubles he faced, and even with the load of guilt he undoubtedly carried after his notorious affair with Bathsheba, he had learned the importance of praising God in both good times and bad. The King James version of the Bible says God inhabits the praises of His people (Psalm 22:3). He dwells where there is praise; He delights in our praise because when we are filled with praise for God, we are no longer self-focused and self-involved.

Praise in Advance

Another important principle of praise is found in 2 Chronicles 20, which is one of my favorite chapters in the Bible. There we read the story of King Jehoshaphat of Judah and his encounter with the enemies of his people, who were out to wipe Judah off the map. This enemy had the manpower and the artillery to do just that.

Through God's prophet Jahaziel, God gave Jehoshaphat and the people of Judah instructions on how they were to fight this great army coming against them. He told them, "Do not be afraid or discouraged because of this vast army. For the battle is not yours, but God's" (2 Chronicles 20:15). So this undermanned and ill-equipped army gathered to march to a battlefield where they were not to fight, but just show up and see how God would deliver them—and look at what happened:

> Jehoshaphat appointed men to sing to the LORD and to praise him for the splendor of his holiness as they went out at the head of the army, saying: "Give thanks to the LORD, for his love endures forever." As they began to sing and praise, the LORD set ambushes against the men of Ammon and Moab and Mount Seir who were invading Judah, and they were defeated (2 Chronicles 20:21-22).

As they marched to the battle, they were praising God in advance even though they had no idea how God was going to fight for them and win this impossible war. I'm quite certain that had I been one of those appointed to lead the army with songs of praise I would have developed laryngitis very quickly! What could singing and praising God do against this forboding enemy? And how foolish they must have felt to march and praise God for victory when, by all accounts, they would be slaughtered?

Notice that "as they began to sing and praise," the enemy was defeated. I am convinced that our battles with guilt can be won when we choose to praise God even before we see the victory, even before our feelings have changed. This is what I believe is meant by "a sacrifice of praise." Hebrews 13:15 instructs us to "continually offer to God a sacrifice of praise—the fruit of lips that confess his name." Praising God when your feelings are lagging behind, when your mind tells you this is crazy, when your heart is still fearful and doubting—that, I believe, is a sacrifice of praise. It is forcing your lips to confess His name. What is the fruit of our lips? Lips produce words, right? So, we must find words that praise God before we see or feel the victory.

Words are very critical. Proverbs 18:21 says, "The tongue has the power of life and death, and those who love it will eat its fruit." What kind of fruit does your tongue produce? What we say to ourselves has a great impact on where we are spiritually because words can bring us life or death. We must learn to speak words of life and refrain from words of death, even if it requires a sacrifice of praise. *Especially* when it requires a sacrifice of praise.

Making Your Own Plan

There is no question God can deliver us from a life plagued with guilt. We can be set free so that our lives glorify Him. Instead of being self-involved, we can live in a way that we are a blessing to all who know us. As long as we labor under a blanket of guilt—whether true or false guilt—we will miss the abundant life. Are you ready to break free? If so, the suggestions in this chapter for managing your guilt will help you because they are based on God's eternal and fail-proof Word.

We looked at a hypothetical woman, Jennifer, and outlined a plan for her to manage her guilt. Now it's time for you to write your own plan so you can become more intentional and biblical in confronting the guilt you struggle with.

Growing Free from Guilt
Your Plan for Guilt Management

1. Are you ready to become more intentional about dealing with your guilt, both true and false?

   ❏ Yes

   ❏ Not sure

   If you're not sure, I encourage you to pray to God and seek some counsel from trusted, godly people if necessary. Or, you can just step out on faith and do it anyway. I promise, it can't hurt!

2. Accept Responsibility

   What sins of the present or past do you need to own up to and confess to God?

   _____

   _____

   _____

   _____

   Write out a prayer of confession, using Jennifer's prayer as a guideline.

   _____

   _____

   _____

   _____

   _____

   _____

   _____

   _____

   (If you are dealing only with false guilt, or with sins that have already been confessed and forgiven, then your prayer needs to be one of confessing your lack of faith in the truths that you have truly been forgiven and that God no longer holds your sins against you. Or, in the case of false guilt, confess that you have believed lies from the enemy instead of believing God, and that this has kept you under the bondage of false guilt for too long.)

3. Changing Your Thought Patterns

   Identify wrong thought patterns and messages that you have allowed into your mind, and find a scriptural antidote for each one:

   Wrong Thought Patterns/Messages   Scriptural Antidote

   _____   _____

   _____   _____

   _____   _____

   _____   _____

   _____   _____

   _____   _____

4. Praise God for Victory

   Choose some specific steps you will take—steps you normally don't take—which will help you to praise God more:

   ❏ I'll sing more praises to God throughout my day, not just at church.

   ❏ I'll recite all that I have to be thankful for more often, especially when I'm feeling discouraged or depressed.

   ❏ I'll memorize some praise verses and quote them frequently.

   ❏ I'll remember to praise God for all the little things that happen every day that I so often take for granted.

   ❏ I'll offer sacrifices of praise and praise God when I don't feel like it at all.

   ❏ I'll praise Him in advance, praising Him by faith for what He will do.

A Closing Word

Now that you've made your way through all these words and pages about guilt, my earnest prayer is that you have come to recognize the damage that guilt feelings can inflict upon your own life, and that you are inspired to fight back!

Because each of us is on our own unique path in our spiritual journey, we must find our own way through the jungle of guilt. No doubt your experience will not be identical to mine or anyone else's. But God's Word gives us principles of truth that never change, regardless of who we are or what we've experienced. Applying those truths to your life may differ in method or technique, but the basic truths themselves will always remain the same. And those truths are our gateway to freedom.

While it is the indwelling Holy Spirit who empowers us to be victorious over guilt, we are still responsible to apply God's truth in a disciplined and consistent way. That word *discipline* is not my favorite word, but I've discovered that to make any progress in my spiritual life, it is always a necessary ingredient.

So, I would exhort and encourage you to be willing to apply the discipline that will unleash the power of God's truth in your life. That means spending quality time in Bible reading and study, in prayer, and in fellowship with other believers who will support you and hold you accountable. None of us ever outgrow our need for those basic spiritual disciplines. I'm certain I could never "walk the talk" without these spiritual disciplines and accountability.

I would be so pleased to hear your story, answer your questions, or help in any way I can. I can be reached at

The Christian Working Woman
PO Box 1210
Wheaton, IL 60189
tcww@christianworkingwoman.org

Appendix

How to Make Sure
You Are a Christian

The focus of this book has primarily been to those who are already a part of the family of God through faith in Jesus Christ. However, I would never want to assume every reader has that assurance. That's why I am including an explanation of what the Bible teaches about becoming a Christian.

If you asked the average person on the street what it means to be a Christian, most would say it has something to do with being a good person. It is a widely held belief that a person can be good enough to be a Christian and therefore, good enough to go to heaven. The standard of what "good enough" is will vary, but most people have that mistaken idea.

The Bible makes it clear that God's standard of "good enough" is perfection—as perfect as God. If you want to become a Christian and be assured that you will go to heaven when you die, you must be as perfect as God, for nothing unholy can enter His presence. You might say, "But no one is perfect!" And there's the rub. "For all have sinned and fall short of the glory of God" (Romans 3:23). If we are all sinners, how can we be as perfect as God?

Here's the answer: We can't, but Jesus is. Jesus, the perfect Son of God, was born to a virgin, which made it possible for Him to never inherit the sin nature passed on through the seed of man. Only Jesus can legitimately claim perfection as a man. He was the eternal Son of God, and He condescended to come to earth and live a perfect life in the body of a man so that He could provide the perfect sacrifice required for imperfect people to be acceptable to a perfect God.

> Your attitude should be the same as that of Christ Jesus: Who, being in very nature God, did not consider equality with God something to be grasped, but made himself nothing, taking the very naure of a servant, being made in human likeness. And being found in appearance as a man, he humbled himself and became obedient to death—even death on a cross! (Philippians 2:5-8)

> The Word [Jesus] became flesh and made his dwelling among us. We have seen his glory, the glory of the One and Only, who came from the Father, full of grace and truth (John 1:14).

By dying on the cross, Jesus became the sacrifice that was foreshadowed by the goat on the Day of Atonement (as explained in chapter 10). Jesus' sacrifice was acceptable to God the Father because His was a perfect sacrifice. And just as the people's sin and guilt were placed on the goat and carried away, so Jesus took our sin and guilt upon Himself at the cross and carried them away. Because of this, God is able and willing to impart the perfection of Jesus to us. We can, as it were, accept this free gift of perfection or righteousness, which comes to us through the sacrifice Jesus made on Calvary. And by accepting it, God credits the righteousness and perfection of Jesus to our account. As 2 Corinthians 5:21 says, "God made him who had no sin to be sin for us, so that in him we might become the righteousness of God."

Before we can accept God's free gift to us, we must recognize our sinful condition, confess our sins to God, and ask Him to give us the gift of the righteousness of Jesus Christ. When "we confess our sins, he is faithful and just and will forgive us our sins and purify us from all unrighteousness" (1 John 1:9).

This confession of sins and acceptance of Jesus as Lord must be intentional. No one is automatically a Christian just because he or she goes to church, is baptized, or comes from a Christian family. Each individual must make this decision personally.

> If you confess with your mouth, "Jesus is Lord," and believe in your heart that God raised him from the dead, you will be saved. For it is with your heart that you believe and are justified, and it is with your mouth that you confess and are saved (Romans 9:10-11).

So if you believe that Jesus was the Son of God and He was raised from the dead after dying for your sins as a perfect sacrifice, and if you confess your sins and you believe in Christ as the only qualified Savior, you are then saved from the punishment that you—and all of us—deserve, which is eternal death and hell.

Just as Jesus was made sin for us and regarded as a sinner when He bore our sin, so are we regarded as righteous and perfect when we receive His free gift of salvation for His righteousness is credited to us. This is utterly amazing and difficult to comprehend. It just seems too good to be true. But it is true, and we must accept it by faith: "It is by grace you have been saved, through faith—and this not from yourselves, it is the gift of God—not by works, so that no one can boast" (Ephesians 2:8-9).

It requires faith on our part to believe that what God has promised He will do. But once you exercise that faith, confess your sins, and accept the righteousness of Jesus as your own, another miracle happens. God gives you a new nature. You are, as Jesus explained to Nicodemus, born again: "I tell you the truth, no one can see the kingdom of God unless he is born again" (John 3:3).

Once you are born again—born from above—God sees you as perfect as Christ because His righteousness is credited to your account. True, you're still not sinless because though you have a new nature, you'll still struggle against the desires of the flesh until you reach heaven. But your new nature gives you the power of God's Holy Spirit. In fact, God's Spirit comes to dwell in you—and that empowers you to be victorious over sin and grow in your knowledge of God's grace and become stronger and stronger in your faith.

One of the evidences that you have been born from above is the new life you have because you have God's Spirit in you: "If anyone is in Christ, he is a new creation; the old has gone, the new has come!" (2 Corinthians 5:17). You will notice new desires, new priorities, new power over sin—a real change inside of you that only God could do. This new life is exciting and is available to all who are willing to confess their sins and accept Christ as Savior.

If you are not totally confident that you have already made this decision, and you do not know for certain that you have this new life in Christ and that your sins are forgiven, you can make that decision now. Here is a prayer you can lift up to God right now to make certain that you are indeed a Christian:

> Dear God,
>
> I know that I am a sinner and there is nothing I can do to save myself. I recognize that I can never be a part of Your family and call You my Father without Your grace and Your mercy. Today I confess my sins to You, and I thank You that You are willing to forgive me. I transfer the guilt of my sin over to Jesus, who paid the price for my sin on the cross, and I accept the free gift of His righteousness, which you will credit to my account. Thank you so much!
>
> I believe that Jesus is the Son of God, that He was raised from the dead, and that because He lives, I too can live with Him in heaven. By faith I accept this, and I thank you that I can now be assured of spending eternity with You in heaven.
>
> Thank You for hearing my prayer. In Jesus' name, amen.

If you have sincerely prayed that prayer or a similar one, here is a promise from Jesus that you can now claim as your own: "I am the resurrection and the life. He who believes in me will live, even though he dies; and whoever lives and believes in me will never die" (John 11:25-26).

If you have made this decision, I would love to hear from you. I want to encourage you in your new faith walk and pray for you. If you desire, you can contact me at:

Mary Whelchel
PO Box 1210
Wheaton, IL 60189

tcww@christianworkingwoman.org

Notes

1. *Random House College Dictionary*, revised edition, s.v. "Delusion."

2. *Random House College Dictionary*, revised edition, s.v. "Conscience."

3. Philip Yancey, *What's So Amazing About Grace?* (Grand Rapids: Zondervan, 1997), p. 12.

4. *Franklin NIV-450 Bible Concordance*, electronic edition (Burlington, NJ: Franklin Electronic Publishers, 2002), s.v. "Guilt."